The Traffic in Women

The Traffic in Women

Human Realities of the
International Sex Trade

Siriporn Skrobanek
Nataya Boonpakdee
Chutima Jantateero

Zed Books Ltd
London and New York

The Traffic in Women was first published by Zed Books Ltd, 7 Cynthia Street, London N1 9JF, UK, and Room 400, 175 Fifth Avenue, New York, NY 10010, USA, in 1997.

Cover designed by Andrew Corbett.
Typeset by Photosetting Services, Yeovil.
Printed and bound in the United Kingdom
by Biddles Ltd, Guildford and King's Lynn.

The right of Siriporn Skrobanek, Nataya Boonpakdee and Chutima Jantateero to be identified as the authors of this work has been asserted by them in accordance with the Copyright, Designs and Patents Act, 1988.

Distributed exclusively in the United States of America by St Martin's Press Inc., 175 Fifth Avenue, New York, NY 10010, USA.

A catalogue record for this book is available from the British Library.

US cataloging-in-publication data has been applied for from the Library of Congress.

ISBN 1 85649 527 2 Cased
ISBN 1 85649 528 0 Limp

Contents

Preface

Tables

Preface

Pain, anger and hope accompanied me throughout the time of writing the final report of the research carried out by the Foundation for Women on the international trafficking of Thai women. The voice of a Thai woman who had resorted to violence to end her slave-like situation in Japan often echoed in my mind:

> Even cattle, after hard work, have time to rest. When they fall sick, they get medical care. But we are human beings. We feel pain and misery like other living creatures. Why did we let her treat us like this?

Why indeed does our human society allow these inhumane, criminal practices to continue? And what makes us neglect this form of gross violation of the basic human rights of women, particularly women from the South? I do hope that by giving a voice to their suffering and to their stories of coercive journeyings, more awareness will be spread, and concrete actions will be taken across national boundaries to put an end to the human tragedies that occur.

Many hands have helped prepare the report for publication. The researchers, Kanchana Bunraksa, Ketkaew Kalong, Pikunthong Sansadi, Waraphon Chamsanit, Sirirat Mahatdechakun, Sida Duangdi, Suchada Sunthonket, Kamrai Khunawut, Jiraphon Saetang, Chorthip Chaicharn, Prinda Chayaboon and Siriporn Chusangkit, spent more than a year on the project, and painstakingly collected the diverse life histories of the women and their families. An essential contribution to the successful outcome of this project has been the willingness of women, who have endured such arduous and painful journeys in their lives, to share their stories and to help others to avoid a similar fate. A number of women's groups that emerged during the action phase of the research project, and their ability to survive after the end of it, gave many of us the hope and encouragement to continue the battle. They showed us that our women need not always be victims, but can take hold of their own lives, and create a better future for themselves and their community.

Members of the advisory task force and core group provided invaluable suggestions during the field research and contributed to the drafting of the report. Three friends of widely differing experience, Darunee Tanwiramanond took an active role in organising the material. Pam Simmons and Jeremy Seabrook helped with editing, and gave comments for the final manuscript, as well as help with publication.

The kind support of the Netherlands Minister for Development Cooperation (Women and Development Section) made it possible for us to embark on this journey of recording how this tragedy could occur in Thailand. Chalermsri Dhamabutra, President of the Foundation for Women, Mary Boesveld and Nelleke van der Vleuten from the Women and Autonomy Centre, Leiden University, are sisters who accompanied us for these three years. Travelling with them was also a search for the true meaning of participation and partnership.

With many such friends, I continue the voyage, in the hope that a day will come soon when this chapter of human tragedy will vanish from contemporary herstory.

Siriporn Skrobanek
Foundation for Women
Bangkok

1

The Trafficked Women of Thailand

Nuj

My name is Nuj and I am 18 years old. I grew up in a village in Mae Sai district, a town on the northern border between Thailand and Burma in Chiang Rai province. Since I was small I remember seeing women – mostly local and those from the ethnic Thai group in Burma's Shan state – wearing thick make-up and beautiful dresses, and walking in and out of the brothels that were mushrooming in the village. The brothels have always been quite busy, especially during festival time, when many Burmese men came over, and the brothel-owners had to bring truck-loads of women from other villages to service them.

My parents love me dearly. They wanted me to have a good education and they always forbade me to look at the women in the brothels. But life in Mae Sai revolved so much around the sex business; daughters are sold to local agents as well as agents from Bangkok. The women who work in the sex trade in Bangkok can send home a lot of money to build big houses and to buy cars. When you see people getting these things, the whole business appears quite attractive… and it wasn't difficult to follow the same path.

As the only daughter, I have always told myself that I must earn enough money to support my poor ageing parents who still have to work very hard to sustain their living. Champa is a local sex worker who has made a fortune working in Bangkok. She always came up to Mae Sai to recruit women to go south. When she asked me to work as her housekeeper in Bangkok, I decided to go with her. Champa told me that I wouldn't have to pay anything for living in Bangkok, and that I would get paid for working. I was 15 then.

During the first three months in Bangkok I was put into an old flat by myself, and had to do all the housework for Champa. One day she took me to a beauty salon and made me wear nice dresses. She took me to work in a massage parlour called 'Darling'. I lived with Champa and her husband, Yongyuth, who beat me and forced me to work as a prostitute. My virginity was sold for 20,000 baht, but I never saw the money.

Throughout the three years I worked in that massage parlour, I never received any money for my body, even though the charge was about 60 baht for the room, and 1,500 baht for the service. Each weekday I had to work from 5 p.m. till midnight, and at weekends my work started at 11 a.m. Each night I had to give service to at least five men – mostly from Saudi Arabia and Japan, as well as Chinese. After work, Champa would bring me back to the flat, and she locked me in the room where I could watch TV. The only holidays I ever had were the religious holidays, when the massage parlours are closed by law.

While working in the parlour I got to know Noi, who worked as the parlour's cashier. Noi felt pity for me, and tried to help me by changing the figures on the receipt of payment from the customers. When a customer gave me a tip of 1,200 baht, Noi would write only 900 baht on the receipt, so that I could keep 300 baht. Noi also helped me to open a bank account, in which I managed to save 5,000 baht. But luck was not on my side. Yongyuth found my wallet one day and saw my Automatic Teller Machine card, which he took after he had beaten me.

My patience was wearing thin, and finally I decided to escape. I had sworn at Yongyuth, and he had beaten me again. I was not afraid. I told him I was going to a beauty salon. I met a man driving by on his motor cycle. He was the head of a gang of construction workers. I asked him to help me escape. Although Yongyuth realised what was happening and followed us in his car, the traffic was quite bad and we got away. That man took me to hide in his office, and helped me contact Noi. Noi suggested I stay with her sister, who happened to know about the emergency home. Noi's sister contacted the emergency home for me. I was then able to study, while working as a cleaner at the guest house run by the home. Noi told me that Champa and Yongyuth found four ethnic women from Mae Sae to work at the parlour after I left.

I'm lucky that I did not contract HIV/AIDS, as I was regularly checked at the clinic. But I realise now how this traumatic experience has affected my life. I used to cut myself, leaving a big wound in my arm. Sometimes I felt desperate, irritated and emotionally hurt. What I have gone through has made me lose confidence in myself. I would love to go back and be with my parents, but I am afraid they are still angry that I left home. For now I plan to take a course to become a hairdresser, so I can work and save some money. Then I'll go home and open my own shop. When that day comes, perhaps all the depressing experiences will fade away from my memory.

Nida

My name is Nida. I am 21 and I come from a village in Chiang Rai province in northern Thailand. There are five of us in the family: my parents, my two younger brothers and myself. I have such a fond memory of my childhood as my father loved me very much. I finished primary school. I was married at 16. Then my father left us to be with another woman; he went so suddenly, it was something I never quite understood. Soon I had to separate from my husband, as our relationship did not go well.

Life was miserable then. I felt sorry for my mother, who still had to work hard without any help from my brothers. I decided to come to Bangkok to work in a factory. After I had been working for two months, I met a woman from my village who had gone to work in Japan. She came back to look for women to work in factories there. I decided to join, although the woman said I would have to repay the expenses, which came to 70,000 baht. I did not have to prepare anything for the trip. On the day of departure the woman told me to travel with a Malaysian man who could speak Thai. I should act as though I were his girlfriend.

When we arrived in Japan the man brought me to a Thai restaurant and negotiated something with the owner. When we left, he told me he was arranging for me to work in that place, but the owner was asking too high a price for my debt – about 700,000 baht. The man thought this was too much, since he had some sympathy for me.

I was sold to a second restaurant, where the owner asked for 400,000 baht for my debt payment. I was forced to work as a prostitute to pay off my debt, and I received only a small amount of pocket money to buy personal items. I could not send any money to my mother. I phoned and told her I was working in a factory in Japan, as I did not want her to know I was actually working as a prostitute.

After four months of working I must have worked enough to pay back almost all my debts, and then I could send some money home. But I was unlucky. I was working as usual one night when a gangster came in. He was attracted to one of the women. She did not want to sleep with him, so he became angry and threatened to close the restaurant. Next morning, about 9 a.m. while I was still asleep, I heard a noise coming from outside. I heard shouting for everyone to escape. I ran to the second floor as one gangster was following me. Out of fear, I jumped from the window. I felt a sharp pain in my back, and I could not move my legs. I was still conscious when my friend took me to the hospital. The first hospital would not admit me because I was a foreigner. At the second hospital, the doctor took my blood for testing, but provided no treatment afterwards. They just let me stay in bed for one week, and told me to go another hospital which had better equipment. Later, I found out that the hospital did not want to give me any treatment because I tested HIV-positive.

Nung: from local brothel to Japanese market

I am 22 years old. I come from a village in Kampangpetch province in upper central Thailand. We used to be quite well-off, because my family had a large piece of land. But my father was a gambler and a drug addict. After he had sold off all the land and the house, my mother took us to live with my aunt.

I went to a local primary school for only a few years before I quit. I was quite big for my age, and my friends always teased me. I didn't like it. A year after I left school an older half-sister of mine, who had moved to live in Aranyaprathet, a town on the Cambodian border, came to visit. She asked if I wanted to travel to Aranyaprathet with her, to go to the annual festival. I agreed to go, and my half-sister gave my mother 500 baht before we left.

There were many women at my half-sister's house, and they seemed to be afraid of my brother-in-law. I did all the housework for her, without pay, but I had free meals and a place to stay. When I had been there five months, there was a festival in town, and my half-sister dressed me up nicely, and introduced me to a fat man she called 'Master'. That man was kind to me. He said that he liked me as if I was one of his children, and he asked me what I would like. On the way back, he drove me to his home. He took me into a room and told me to sleep while he lay down next to me. I was not afraid, but felt secure. I was falling asleep when I realised what that Master was trying to do. I tried to escape, but he punched me in the stomach and I lost consciousness.

From then on I was forced to be a prostitute. That man was the Master of my half-sister and her husband, who worked in the brothel. Half the payment for my body was taken every time by these people, so I could make no savings. After three years of working there I decided to go to another province to work in a bar where I could earn enough to send money home; my mother would then be able to buy some land. When my half-sister found out about my job, she followed me to work in the same bar and became my agent, making money out of the service

I gave. I could not bear this situation, and wanted to quit the job and go home. I got married; a local man. I had one son. I went to live, with my in-laws, but they did not like me. I left and went back to work with my half-sister in the bar.

While working I met a man who asked me if I wanted to go to work in Japan. I contacted a company, and they arranged all the travel documents, but I could not get the permit to travel. I changed my name to obtain a visa. I went to Japan with a Thai man, travelling as his girlfriend. He sold me to a restaurant for 300,000 baht. Although I had to move from place to place to work, I was never beaten. There was also one gangster who always came to see me, and took me out with him, even when he went to make deals in the drug trade.

After working in Japan for five months I began to feel ill. I often had a pain in my stomach and I felt that it was getting bigger. I thought I was pregnant, so I asked my friend to kick me in the stomach to abort the baby, but nothing came out. The pain became so severe that I could not work. I decided to go back to Thailand, but I did not get any help from the Thai Embassy. Someone told me to contact a private agency called Mizura for assistance. They helped by contacting the Foundation for Women in Bangkok, who arranged for my travel. I came back to Thailand and stayed at the Shelter for Women run by the Foundation. A member of staff took me to hospital for an examination. I was diagnosed as having cancer of the ovaries. The doctor told me I needed an operation. After the operation I stayed at the Shelter for a while before returning to Kampangpetch.

I do not want to go back to work in Japan again, although the bar owner told me I am always welcome to return. Now I only want to live with my son and my mother, and find some funding to start a small business at home.

2

The Basis for the Foundation for Women's Research into the Trafficking of Thai Women

Migration and Trafficking

Migration from the countryside to towns and cities and from one country to another has, throughout history, been a significant form of population movement. Vast migrations have always occurred, whether as a result of military conquest, natural disaster or famine. Most have been involuntary – notably at the time of the slave trade – forcible migrations which have changed the face of the world. Brazil is a country the majority of whose population comprises descendants of slaves, while Liberia in West Africa was founded as a state for freed slaves. The Caribbean and the Americas have been marked by slavery, and the overwhelmingly black underclass in the United States testifies to the enduring influence of this form of traffic in human beings. Within the industrial era, the migration of labour has been an essential part of economic growth and development, while the age of imperialism shifted large groups of people half-way round the world in pursuit of its objectives. People from Tamil Nadu were sent by the British as indentured labour to work in the rubber plantations of Malaya, while a population of 'coolies' and labourers modified the ethnic composition of many countries; indigenous peoples everywhere were forced to migrate from their forests, fishing-grounds and farmlands because the conquerors laid claim to the lands they occupied.

In the mid-19th century, Thailand was already touched by these movements. Chinese labourers were brought in to boost production, following a 'free trade' agreement with the United Kingdom. Today,

Thailand encourages temporary migrants from Burma, Laos and Cambodia to work in the construction and fishing industries.

The 1948 Universal Declaration of Human Rights (Article 13) states that '...everyone has the right to leave any country including his (*sic*) own'. The 1968 International Covenant on Civil and Political Rights (Article 12), however, sets limits by stating that these rights shall be subject to restrictions provided by law when required for national security, peace and public order, public health or morals, or the rights and freedoms of others.

Although migration is a basic human right, it is circumscribed by many qualifications and restrictions set by governments. These are usually flexible. When the industrialised countries experienced labour shortages at times of full employment in the 1950s and 1960s, Europe did not hesitate to recruit workers from Turkey, India, Pakistan, Bangladesh, the Caribbean, Morocco and Algeria. Even for those who viewed such migrations as 'temporary' – such as the German attitude to 'Gastarbeiter' – it has proved extremely difficult even to speak of repatriation, even though there are now 4 million unemployed in Germany. When the North was importing labour, the countries of the South encouraged its own people to migrate.

Thailand actively encouraged emigration from 1977. The government supported and supervised job-placement agencies. At first, these jobs were mainly for men in the Middle East and neighbouring countries. Significant numbers of women began to leave only in the mid-1980s, and the government evolved no clear policy towards them. The patterns of female migration appear to follow those set by men, although, of course, the work available is different. Women are restricted to the domestic and service sector. A dominant element in this is illegal, unofficial migration to serve the international sex industry. As the migration of Thai women as sex workers has grown, it has evolved into the organised and highly efficient international trafficking of women.

Human trafficking is an aspect of migration. In the contemporary world, it is primarily women who are trafficked. Earlier this century, this was recognised by the League of Nations (forerunner of the United Nations) in a number of agreements designed to combat the sale of women and children. This was better known as the 'white slave trade', because if focused mainly on white women forced into prostitution.

In 1949, the UN General Assembly approved a new Convention to replace the earlier international conventions of 1904, 1919, 1921 and 1933. This was called the Convention for the Suppression of Traffic in Persons and of the Exploitation of Prostitution of Others. It has so far been ratified by 70 countries. Its function is to combat the trading in persons for the purpose of prostitution. It does not include trafficking for other purposes, and does not cover all contemporary forms of trafficking.

Thailand and Traffic in Women

Traffic in women was first observed in Thailand following the immigration of Chinese labourers in the mid-19th century. A significant number of women followed the flow of migrants, some against their will, for marriage or prostitution. A 1933 report from the League of Nations recorded Thailand as a receiving country for foreign women. In 1928, in compliance with the international convention, Thailand introduced an Act against Traffic in Women and Girls.

In 1960, the Act for the Abatement of Prostitution was passed. Based on the 1949 Convention, it sought to abolish prostitution. All activities associated with prostitution, except the selling of sex *per se*, became illegal. State regulation of brothels ceased and procurers were to be punished. But recruitment of women and children into prostitution, including the traffic across borders, continues. Compared with the trade in women earlier this century, it now appears to be more systematic and the conduits through which it operates more efficient.

In the late 1960s, the sex industry in Thailand expanded in response to the establishment of many US military bases in the region. After the Vietnam War, this continued through civilian tourism. Contact with foreign men opened up possibilities of migration for some women. Overseas labour markets, on the other hand, offered only limited job choices for women, invariably in the service sector, as domestics and entertainers.

Migration serving the international sex industry developed through the 1980s, as demand for foreign sex workers grew in the clubs and bars of Europe, and later, of East Asia. These workers labour under great difficulties, because their residence as well as their work are often illegal. They are frequently exploited and deceived by false promises, and it is in this context that trafficking in women for prostitution can flourish.

Action Research on Traffic in Women

Recognising the need for more decisive action to combat trafficking of women from Thailand, the Foundation for Women (Thailand) and the Women's Autonomy Centre of Leiden University (the Netherlands) agreed to co-operate on a three-year study of trafficking. Begun in 1993 with the support of the Netherlands Foreign Ministry, the aim of the project was to produce detailed evidence which would serve as a basis for policy recommendations and practical measures. It was also hoped that the project would develop a research methodology that could be replicated elsewhere. The overall aims of the study were:

• to develop and improve the strategies for governmental and non-governmental agencies in resisting traffic in women;
• to make policy recommendations for more effective co-operation between government and non-government sectors in this area;
• to assist international co-operation in the fight against traffic in women, specifically through the development of a research methodology for comparative studies in other countries;
• to encourage greater participation by village women in putting a stop to traffic in women from their area.

The project was divided into two phases: the first ten months to be spent collecting data in the target areas; the second ten months to test strategies against trafficking, involving the participation of local women. The study was based on two fundamental ideas:

• Traffic in women is an aspect of transnational migration, and is a global issue. The study must, therefore, examine the evolving international division of labour, the migration policies of sending and receiving countries, and the impact of this on female labour migration, both nationally and internationally.
• Traffic in women is a grave violation of human rights, and is a contemporary form of slavery. It is not simply a problem for the individual victim, but an international issue which cannot be separated from global economic, social and political institutions.

Target areas

Information on the migration and traffic in women was collected in urban and rural communities, based on interviews with a total of 131 women. Bangkok and Pattaya were selected as representative of major urban centres to which rural women characteristically migrate. These cities also attract many sex tourists. There are a number of governmental and non-governmental agencies in Bangkok and Pattaya which help women. These include the Emergency Home for Women and the Home for Battered Women in Bangkok, and the Fountain of Life Centre in Pattaya. In collaboration with these agencies, the researchers interviewed 28 women and their families in Bangkok and 26 in Pattaya. The interviews were designed to gain an insight into the mechanics of migration and trafficking, the working conditions and problems encountered in the sex industry, and the help available to the women.

In the rural areas, the researchers interviewed women from four villages. In northern Thailand, 11 women and their families from 'Soi Dao', Chiang Mai province, and 32 from 'Rim Mon', Chiang Rai province, agreed to be interviewed. In north-eastern Thailand, there were 22 interviewees from 'Ton Yang' in Nong Khai province, and 12 from 'Khon Na' in Udon Thani province. The names of the villages have been changed. These interviews were concerned with the development of trafficking, with a comparison between the villages and the two regions, and with the views of the village people on how to deal with the issues. The areas for research were chosen because of the experience of the Foundation for Women with migration and prostitution, and in each area a local contact helped with the interviews.

In the second phase of the study – to test strategies of resistance to trafficking – the villages were different. In the north, researchers worked only in 'Rim Mon' village. In the north-east, they worked in 'Ton Yang', Nong Khai province, and a village close to 'Khon Na', 'Na Thong', Udon Thani province.

Soi Dao, established about 200 years ago, is the oldest of the four villages which supplied data for the study. It is also the furthest from the provincial business and administrative centre (see Table 2.1). Ton Yang is closest to its provincial centre and has the highest population. It has more emigrants than the others. All except Khon Na have good roads to the provincial town.

Table 2.1:   Details of villages where data was collected

Village	Age (years)	Distance from provincial centre (km)	Population		
			male	female	total
Rim Mon (N)	125	32	477	494	971
Soi Dao (N)	200	101	352	320	672
Ton Yang (NE)	100	15	830	881	1711
Khon Na (NE)	65	53	266	249	515

The main source of livelihood is agriculture, chiefly rice cultivation. During the period of the study, major irrigation projects were under way in Ton Yang and Soi Dao. Some villagers complained that their agricultural land had been taken by the state for irrigation channels and basins. In the north, in the off-season, additional income derives from the sale of minor crops and wage labour in local tobacco factories. In the north-east, supplementary income is made from the sale of handicrafts – mats and baskets – and from seasonal work in the urban centres.

These villages have a history of poverty and migration. In the two northern villages, female migration is higher than male, whereas in the north-east the reverse is true. There is evidence from Soi Dao that girls have been recruited for prostitution since at least 1971. In Rim Mon, the first example of migration for prostitution took place in 1976. Recruiters were local people, and these now include former prostitutes. This report shows the effect on these villages of two decades of migration for the sex industry.

In Ton Yang and Khon Na in the north-east, there has been rural–urban migration since the mid-1960s. Migration for prostitution appeared only in the mid-1970s. Compared to the north, there was a weaker link between migration and the sex industry.

3

Migration

The idea of migration covers various forms of movement of peoples, from forcible transfers of population, such as the ousting of the Aboriginals of Australia or the native peoples of the USA, to the active recruitment of workers in order to answer sometimes temporary labour shortages, such as present-day planeloads of Bangladeshis and Indonesians in transit to the plantations of Malaysia or the construction sites of the Gulf.

As the global economy becomes more integrated, we see more and more people working far from their place of origin; and since the trajectory of such displacements is usually from poor countries to rich, it is only to be expected that the wealthy countries seek to exclude people they now refer to as 'economic migrants', a term which delegitimises their efforts to enter Europe or the USA, and leads, increasingly, to their repatriation. While goods and money cross national boundaries with ever greater ease, this is not extended to the other major factor of production, labour.

People will naturally seek to circumvent such arbitrary restrictions, and will find a way of crossing boundaries, through which ways can always be found, whether legally or unofficially. This leads to more and more people living in conditions of secrecy, as hidden or clandestine inhabitants of the countries where they labour; which, in turn, exposes them to greater levels of exploitation and ill-treatment, against which they are often without redress.

It is only when some spectacular incident occurs – such as a group of Sri Lankans suffocating to death in intolerable heat in the back of a truck in Hungary, or the plight of an abused or sexually molested maidservant who runs away from her employers in Jeddah or Paris, or illegal workers locked into a factory in California being burnt to death – that the conscience of the rich is sometimes stirred. For the most part, the world of unofficial migrants remains difficult to reach.

If this is true of male migrants, it is especially true of women. Historically, the pattern of women's migration differs from that of men. Women do not come from the same social background. They have other reasons for leaving, their means of travel and destination are not the same. Earlier, most women migrants went as family members or to get married, while men tended to migrate independently, for reasons of employment. Independent female migration has escaped accurate documentation; perhaps because women have always appeared less threatening than men to the receiving country.

In many ways women are more likely than men to maintain contact with the family, and to continue to send money home, especially if they leave children behind. In the decision as to which member of the family leaves, it is increasingly women who go. Indeed, in the global flow from South to North, there are now as many women migrants as men. These decisions are also governed by the circumstances in the country to which they go, such as opportunities for women in the labour market, discriminatory laws and civic status (in many countries, a woman's legal status depends on her husband), as well as labour and migration laws (Chant 1992: 203).

Millions of people who have moved from the South have done so as a consequence of globalisation. The world economy is still controlled and manipulated by the G-7, the periodic meeting of whose leaders is referred to as the 'global economic summit'. These leaders accept no responsibility for the workings of economic forces, over which they paradoxically, and when it suits them, claim to have no influence. Mass communications also convey an imagery of luxury and affluence to the people of the South, which beckons them, sometimes with disastrous results, as those who encounter discrimination, racism and exploitation frequently testify. In the 1960s, the presence of migrants in Western Europe was accepted, on the grounds that 'they are doing the kind of work that no one else wants to do'; this did not prevent them from being accused of 'taking our jobs', as soon as unemployment recurred.

Until recently, the international labour market has favoured jobs characteristically done by men, such as construction and industrial work. Even work in commerce, and some forms of domestic service, especially in the Gulf, was offered to men. This is now changing. More women than men are now going abroad in search of a livelihood from some Asian countries. The great majority are domestic workers (Chant and Radcliffe 1992: 8). In Europe, the USA and Australia, migrant women may also work in 'female' industries, such as garment manufacture (Chant and Radcliffe 1992: 8–9). In this way, traditional gender divisions of labour are reinforced by the international labour market.

Policies to control migration and to protect the rights of migrants have reflected this gender bias, and have been concentrated in the formal sector where men predominate. Women have become invisible, and female migration has been easily overlooked. All this only makes easier the exploitation and abuse of women.

Women's Work

Migrants have readily performed labour which local people have come to regard as demeaning or dirty. For migrants, the economic gain outweighs low social status (Massey et al. 1993: 421). Many women university graduates from the Philippines work as domestic helpers abroad, since work for which they are trained is not available. To labour as dancers or prostitutes is rarely the first choice of women working overseas. Men face similar limitations, but there is a wider range of work on offer, and, unlike women, they sometimes have the opportunity to upgrade their skills.

Prostitution, especially at the lower end of the market, has become more international since the 1970s. In the Netherlands, for example, there was a shift from white Dutch women to Asian, African and Latin American women in the red-light districts. More recently, women from Eastern Europe have been joining this cosmopolitan labour force.

Many factors increase the demand for migrant women in the sex trade. Prostitution is often illegal or subject to discriminatory public order regulations. Local women will no longer enter the business, either because of the social stigma, or because of growing awareness of the health risks. Some move into the higher end of the market, with limited clientele, or in clubs or escort agencies. How far migrants compete with local women in this market is not clear.

Migration for prostitution is also linked to male migration, both nationally and internationally. The cities of India, for instance, are overwhelmingly male. The brothels of Bombay and Calcutta teem with young women from Nepal, the hills and tribal areas, to service the desire of lone males, isolated from wives and families. Many of these women were initially abducted or kidnapped, some to serve in closed houses, where they remain as a form of bonded labour.

Prostitution is also influenced by popular ideas of 'exotic' women. In the West, these may embody stereotypes of submissiveness, on the one hand, and lewdness on the other. In any case, all kinds of licence are granted with 'foreign' women, which would not be tolerated with local women. Sex tourism strengthens these stereotypes, and raises demand for 'exotic' women, thus leading to an intensification of trafficking and clandestine migration (Van de Vleuten 1991: 41).

Marriage of a daughter to a foreigner is sometimes seen by the poor as a means of enhancing family wealth. Such marriages are 'often a thin veil for cheap domestic and sexual services' (Chant and Radcliffe 1992: 8–9). There are many examples of Thai women who discover after their 'marriage' to Europeans, whom they may have met as sex tourists, that their sexual services are being sold by their husbands. In Germany and Japan, marriage bureaux advertise in newspapers and farmers' magazines. Male farmers are in a weak position in the marriage market, since their isolation and the hard work of farming offer unattractive prospects to local women (Chant and Radcliffe 1992: 9).

Women migrants, then, are often sequestered in private homes, or reduced to the informal or semi-legal sector. This creates dependency on middlemen, employers or husbands. Most migrant workers in the sex industry exist in a legal twilight, without proper papers, unprotected by the law of the country where they live.

Migration Sustained

Other elements contribute to the pressures to migrate. Poor families are acutely aware of neighbours who grow rich, and are often ready to follow the same path (Massey et al. 1993: 439). Easy and cheap travel also facilitate migration. Word of mouth plays an important role in the decision to leave home. Family members, friends and acquaintances make it appear easy, and they know how to go about it. Clusters of people from the same place settle in the same foreign city: for example, Bangladeshis in East London have, for the most part, come from Sylhet. Migration becomes self-perpetuating (Massey et al. 1993: 449). Over time, the profile of migrants changes to become more characteristic of the overall sending community, rather than just part of it. The Research and Action Project on Traffic in Women confirms that word of mouth plays a major role in determining who migrates. Kritaya Archavanitkul concludes that such networks are more powerful than the socio-economic status of families in deciding which young rural people go and where they go to (Archavanitkul and Guest 1993: 16).

Having migrated once, the individual is likely to migrate again, since migration alters people's sensibility and values, which prevent them from being able to return to the village (Sripraphai and Sripraphai 1994; Massey et al. 1993: 452). Those who are known to have worked as prostitutes may find themselves rejected by the community.

International migration is further influenced by the agencies and organisations which make money from it. These include travel agents, both legal and illegal, those forging passports and visas, and those

creating bogus marriages and counterfeit papers. The pressure of such
influences is so strong that migration flows are scarcely amenable to
control by official policy (Massey et al. 1993: 451).

Dependency and Exploitation

A high level of dependency is common among migrants, whether on
family members, friends, recruiting agents, employers or state authorities.
Dependency is increased where restrictions on migration are enforced
and work is illegal. This makes exploitation more likely. It is reported
that tens of thousands of people, mainly men, from mainland China,
are smuggled into the US each year by organised crime syndicates. They
pay US$35,000–50,000 for this 'service'. The debt incurred is equivalent
to a hundred years' salary at home, and is paid back by five years' labour,
seven days and nights a week in sweatshops, restaurants and laundries
(Stalker 1994: 36).

Exploitation of migrant workers is commonplace in domestic and sex
work. Often illegal, and requiring minimal skills, most domestic work is
performed in private homes, and this seclusion increases the likelihood
of economic exploitation and sexual harassment. A Filipino diplomat in
Saudi Arabia described Filipina domestic workers as 'modern-day slaves'.
Sixty per cent of the 3.5 million Filipino workers overseas are based in
Saudi Arabia.

Migrant women in the commercial sex trade may work voluntarily
or against their will. Bonded labour is widespread. Women are often
duped, unaware that sexual services are part of their job. Migrants are
easy to control – their legal status is doubtful, they lack language skills,
and have little knowledge of their rights. They may be compelled to work
in confined spaces, with little freedom of movement outside the workplace. Where deception has been employed to induce them to migrate,
this is, in our view, the equivalent of trafficking.

Traffic in Women

The extent of trafficking of women has been obscured by the general
flow of migration. The documentation of women moving independently
of men and families has been inadequate. There are records of country
girls going to London and Paris at the end of the 19th century to work
as domestics or prostitutes. In Victorian London, domestic servants
constituted the largest single category of employees; those who lost their
livelihood often gravitated to the sex industry; and indeed, many of them

did lose their work in consequence of the attentions of the master of the house in which they served.

As part of the migration of Chinese labourers early in the 20th century, Chinese girls were trafficked to work in brothels on the west coast of the US (Bullough and Bullough 1991: 7). Between 1919 (when Thailand first signed the Bowring 'free trade' treaty) and 1929, the number of Chinese migrant labourers rose from about 200,000 a year to 450,000. Over the same period, the proportion of women among them rose from 21 to 29 per cent. In 1933, a League of Nations report listed Thailand as a country of destination for impoverished women and girls: it estimated at 2–3,000 a year the number of Chinese women brought to Thailand for prostitution. They worked in brothels owned for the most part by resident Chinese. Of the 151 registered brothels in Bangkok at that time, 126 were Chinese-owned.

One of the most notorious episodes in the 20th century concerned the 'comfort-women' forcibly transported to Japan from neighbouring countries to serve the military in the Second World War. It took more than 40 years for the scale of these traffickings to become clear, and for the Japanese government to acknowledge the atrocities committed against these women. Trafficking of white women was also the subject of popular literature and films in the early 20th century. Western women kidnapped and taken to the harems of Arab and African rulers may have fed the indignation of Western racists, but little accurate information is available (Van der Vleuten 1991: 7). Since the 1970s, the number of women going abroad for work has increased. This has coincided with a rise in trafficking. Just as Chinese labourers came into Thailand early this century, now many Burmese are crossing the border in search of work in construction and fishing. Women and girls are being trafficked to brothels to service this flow of migrants (Asia Watch 1994).

Traffic in women has always been linked to prostitution, and was first recognised at the end of the 19th century. In Victorian England, prostitution – including that of children – was widespread, but was regarded as being beyond the concern of polite society, which chose to ignore it. Social reformers focused on the women themselves – 'fallen women', as they were called. Even Gladstone, who later became Prime Minister, went on excursions of dubious propriety through the streets of London in his 'mission' to reclaim such women. Any talk of the state regulating prostitution was regarded as condoning 'moral decay' (Van der Vleuten 1991: 17–22).

There are, of course, forms of forcible abduction other than for prostitution. The UN Expert Group on Measures to Eradicate Violence against Women stated that traffic in women includes forced prostitution, forced domestic labour, false marriages, clandestine employment and false adoption (STV 1993). To understand the position of trafficked women requires multiple perspectives. They must be seen as migrant workers, as prostitutes and as women in a male-dominated society (Wijers 1994). Force and deception, however, are the key to the issue. 'Force', as defined by the 1994 Utrecht Conference on Traffic in Persons, may mean an act or threat of violence, or any other act, or the abuse of authority, the abuse of processes of law, the use of extortion or coercion, or deception. Trafficking is not an isolated action, but a process, whereby women are coerced into a position in which they believe they have no choice. In addition to this definition of the Utrecht Conference, we believe that the idea of traffic in women must be widened to include the luring or conveying of women, under false promises or bogus identities, to places where they will be compelled to work in slave-like conditions.

If trafficking is to be understood as a distortion of the normal process of migration, it is essential to identify and outlaw the elements of violence, coercion and deceit involved in it. In doing so, we must take care not to add further disadvantages to women migrants, for the migration of women is a survival strategy for many households and women in the countries of the South. These are not problems of individual women. Traffic in women has its origin in the economic exploitation of female labour and sexuality, and is a structural problem. Many social actors are involved: parents, traffickers, adult males, government officers, policy makers. To tackle the issue requires strong political will, at national and international level. It also needs local women with experience of migration and trafficking to be involved in developing strategies of resistance.

Participatory Feminist Research

Official action aimed at preventing forced prostitution and trafficking, or in providing assistance to women forced into prostitution, has too often been based on what the authorities think about the women, rather than on the views, needs and wishes of the women themselves. This may be to some extent due to the difficulty in maintaining contact with women sex workers, particularly where they are kept in virtual seclusion by brothel owners. A second factor is the assumption that experts from outside know best. Prostitution is still widely perceived as indecent and immoral, which is not how the customers of prostitutes are seen. Prostitutes are also perceived as objects of pity, victims who need help. Both of these positions make it impossible to work with sex workers or trafficked women on equal terms. A similarly unhelpful position is adopted by those groups which aim to abolish prostitution.

It is a basic understanding of the Research and Action Project on Traffic in Women that the most just and effective work can be done only in partnership with the women affected by trafficking. The rest of this book documents the course and results of this project.

4

Migration and the Trade in Women in Thailand

Among the rights of individuals according to the Universal Declaration of Human Rights (Article 13) are various rights and freedoms to movement and residence, both within and outside their countries. These include the right to leave and return to any country, including their own. Such rights are fundamental, and are restated in the International Covenant on Civil and Political Rights (Article 12).

In the light of this, it has been suggested that a right to migrate exists under international law. Whether one has the right freely to enter any country at will remains a contentious issue. It is usually seen as the right of sovereign nations to restrict and to refuse entry to non-nationals; and this right is deployed in the North particularly against applicants from developing countries.

It cannot be repeated too often that the issue of migration cannot be separated from the workings of the global economy. The 'integration' of the vast majority of countries into a single global economy has had far-reaching consequences. From the 1950s until the 1980s, there was a vast increase in the export of cheap labour from the South to the North. In Britain, for example, the National Health Service and urban transport departments actively recruited workers in the Caribbean; tens of thousands of people from the Indian sub-continent worked round the clock in shifts to keep the textile factories of Lancashire and Yorkshire competitive. More than a million Turks went to Germany as 'guest-workers', while as many from Algeria, Morocco and Tunisia sought a livelihood in France. Migrants into the United States, both official and unofficial, have, for generations, supplied a continuous stream of cheap labour.

As economic recession took hold in many industrial nations, particularly in Europe, both at the beginning and again at the end of the 1980s, attempts were made not only to stem the flow of labour, but also to prevent dependants of established migrants from joining them. As countries came out of recession, unemployment remained obdurately high. New technology increasingly displaced manual and unskilled labour, and, at the same time, much manufacturing industry relocated from Europe to the South. As this happened, xenophobia and racism, never far from the surface in Europe, became more evident. Far-right parties gained votes in France, Belgium, Austria and Germany. Criticisms of migrants and their children became less muted. It was objected that they did not fit in with 'our culture'. The children of migrants, it was alleged, are disproportionately likely to turn to crime. 'There is no room' became a familiar cry. The homes and hostels of migrants and refugees in Germany became the targets of outrages, while even the more liberal countries in Europe, such as Sweden, began to experience organised racism.

The need to import foreign labour into industrialised economies has now vanished. This, in part, reflects the tendency of transnational companies to move their operations 'off shore', that is, to seek cheap labour *in situ*, rather than require the cumbersome process of mass migration. This has the added advantage of circumventing labour laws and welfare obligations in the wealthier countries. Only limited forms of labour are now imported into Europe, mainly domestic workers, whose remittances still make a significant contribution to some countries' economies. In the Philippines, for instance, 17 per cent of households depend upon income from abroad. The Labour Minister of Indonesia expressed his hope that by the year 2000 there would be 2.5 million Indonesians working abroad, from whose income the country would make a net gain of US$10 billion annually. Most of these workers would not be in Western Europe, Japan or the US, but in booming countries in Asia such as Malaysia or South Korea.

Migration nevertheless continues to the countries of the North. The difference now is that most of this is unofficial, undocumented and illegal. Would-be immigrants arrive with a visitor's visa and simply go underground. There are networks of compatriots willing to give them shelter and conceal them. Most of these work in the private sector: in small factories, restaurants (where raids by police and immigration officials sometimes find 10 or 20 Bangladeshis or Turks living in the workplace, sleeping in the kitchens of a restaurant, or in a cellar which is also a factory), and in agriculture, where fruit-picking is often done on a daily basis for cash in hand.

It can be argued that globalisation has, despite the efforts to close loopholes, actually increased the flow of migrant labour. At the very least, it has increased the desire to migrate and the pressure upon people in the South to do so. In an era of allegedly free markets, to permit goods, capital and rich people to move freely around the world, while preventing labour from doing so, appears both hypocritical and unjust.

Japan, for instance, has very strict immigration laws, but this has not prevented migrants from entering the country. The reputation of Japan as a supremely wealthy country, with limitless opportunities to get rich, is known throughout the world. Its exports and its investment in South and East Asia speak of a world of luxury and ease. The showrooms of Japanese cars, televisions, videos and photographic equipment in Bangkok, Jakarta, Manila, Dhaka tell their own story. Media images of the lifestyle of the rich serve as a magnet to the impoverished in the slums of the cities and the ruined farmlands of the South.

There is a savage irony in the immigration policies of the industrialised countries: they invoke the sovereignty of the nation state on the one hand, yet speak of 'global integration' on the other. Restrictive immigration policies, combined with a global market that uproots, disturbs and destroys traditional patterns of living in the South, combine to create an increase in efforts by the poor to pass through the closed borders of the countries of the rich. One major by-product of this has been the rise in an illegal and damaging trade in human beings. This trade has become more sophisticated. The global market economy casts a lengthening shadow of illicit transactions. To the list of forbidden articles of trade – cocaine and heroin, endangered plants, rare butterflies, pandas and rhinos, gold and precious stones – we must add the enslavement of women.

Thai Women and Migration

Rural–urban migration is a long-established pattern in all the countries of the South. The nature of migration is now changing. In Thailand, the number of men going to the towns and cities is now exceeded by that of women. In a 1993 survey of recent migrants to Bangkok from the countryside, 100 of the 187 migrants were women (Archavanitkul and Guest 1993: 2). An earlier survey in 1992 suggested that more men than women move between one rural area and another. This difference is a reflection of the locality where work is most readily available for men and women.

In traditional societies, women were rarely encouraged to leave home, or even to move beyond the limits of the household. It has been the privilege of men to go in search of a livelihood, to seek a better living away from home, to look to wider horizons. The industrialisation of Thailand in the late 20th century has disrupted many cultural and social traditions. Its impact on the family has been far-reaching. For more than

30 years, Thailand has had National Social and Economic Development Plans. These have given priority to the industrial sector, especially those industries which are export-oriented. Tourism and the service sector have only recently been given the same attention as manufacturing industry. Since the 1970s, the export of labour has formed part of official development strategy, because the remittances of migrants contribute towards foreign exchange, and because migrants represent the commitment of the nation to participate in the international economy (Pongsapich 1994: 2–4).

These development priorities have adversely affected those in the agricultural sector. Many rural people left their homes for the big cities (Heyzer 1986). This rural–urban migration was sometimes temporary. For some it was seasonal. One of the reasons why the official population of Bangkok appears so low is that it is a city of migrants, some commuting on a daily basis, others returning to their native village when help is needed in the paddy-fields.

The economic growth-rate of Thailand reached 11.6 per cent in 1990. In 1993 it was still 8.4 per cent (Bank of Thailand 1995). Improvements in transport and communications have brought city life closer to the countryside, which is no longer regarded as remote. If Bangkok is a city of country people, the villages are full of semi-urban peasants. Rural people have increasingly taken part in the development of Thailand by sending members of the family to work in Bangkok. In central Thailand in particular, women had fewer opportunities than men in agricultural work. The need for cheap female labour in light industry offered them openings in the city (Archavanitkul and Guest 1993: 4).

One thing that has not changed throughout the upheavals of industrialisation is women's responsibility for the care of children and elderly parents. One of the consequences of migration is that the care of young children has increasingly passed to grandmothers, while parents work in the cities or overseas. For women, the sense of indebtedness to their parents remains strong, and is fulfilled by remittances home, a consolation for their absence. Men's sense of indebtedness can be discharged more easily through short-term ordination as Buddhist monks, which confers merit upon their parents. Youngest daughters in particular are expected to take care of their parents in the later years of their lives (Potter 1976). A study of households in north Thailand found that, on average, 28 per cent of household income came from absent daughters (Archavanitkul and Guest 1993: 4).

Kritaya Archavanitkul, in a study of trafficking in women, concluded that work in the sex industry is one of the few channels open to women with low levels of education which permits them to make money rapidly and in substantial quantities (Archavanitkul 1993: 15).

International Migration of Thai People

From 1983 onwards, the number of Thais working overseas jumped significantly, partly as a result of the government policy of exporting labour. The most popular destinations for women workers were Hong Kong and Japan (see Table 4.1).

Table 4.1 Thai migrant labourers registered with the Department of Labour 1990–93

Destination	Male	Female	Total
South East Asia	96,594	36,282	132,876
Middle East	69,048	3,695	72,743
Africa	1,618	73	1,691
Europe/North America	6,076	3,852	9,928
Total	173,336	43,902	217,238

Countries to which more women migrate

Hong Kong	815	19,498	20,313
South Korea	68	160	228
Japan	9,542	9,779	19,321
Germany	412	704	1,116
United Kingdom	319	326	645

Source: Pongsapich 1994: 12

In 1993, the Thai Embassy in Japan estimated that there were between 80,000 and 100,000 Thai women working in the Japanese sex industry (Archavanitkul 1993). Kritaya Archavanitkul (1993) divides international migration of Thai labour into four periods:

• 1967–77: the start of labour migration. Migrant workers received relatively high wages and labour recruiting agencies paid all expenses.
• 1978–81: a rise in demand for migrant labour abroad. More employment agencies sprang up, but increasingly the migrants themselves were expected to pay expenses. There were few reports

    of fraud or deceit.

- 1982–87: demand for migrant labour slackened while the supply increased. Fees rose, and it was reported that workers mortgaged their rice farms to enable them to pay the commission charges. Deceit by recruiters became more common. Many workers arrived to discover their earnings were lower than promised.
- 1988–the present: employment agencies make even more extravagant promises to entice potential workers. Workers pay commission to the agents of 80,000–250,000 baht (US$3,300–10,400). Many workers are deceived by agents and employers. The government continues to encourage the export of labour.

Official government policy on the export of labour, first recorded in the Fifth National Social and Economic Development Plan, 1982–86, was formulated only after the increase in emigration (Pongsapich 1994: 14). Following the enunciation of government policy, migrant workers experienced a decrease in pay and growing problems with migration. The export of labour is now the second highest foreign exchange earner.

From 1976 to 1990, there was a five-fold increase in remittances from overseas workers, from 485 million baht to 24.9 billion baht (US$20 million to US$1 billion). Most of this comes in the form of Japanese yen. Twenty per cent of all migrant workers are women, who contributed 4.95 billion baht to the national economy in 1990 (about US$200 million).

Labour laws should be standardised to ensure equal rights and identical working conditions in all workplaces, regardless of the origins of workers. As Kritaya Archavanitkul details in her study of migrant labour, conditions for many such workers fall well below legal minimum standards. Low wages, high debts and deception over working conditions are commonplace. In some countries, the worst-paid, lowest-status jobs are reserved for migrants, who are subject to racism from officials, employers and the public alike. These experiences adversely affect the mental and physical health of the workers.

Women and International Migration

Discrimination against women is widespread in Thailand, as may be seen from the limited choices of employment open to women. Migrant women workers are doubly discriminated against, and the only work available to them is as unskilled labourers, domestic helpers or commercial sex workers.

Thai women who seek work as prostitutes in the industrialised countries are motivated mainly by the need for money, and secondarily by the desire to travel. The historical experience of migration among women mirrors that of male labourers: at first, returns were high, but as competition grew, agents and traders, forced to compete, became less scrupulous.

The income from sexual services offered by Thai women abroad was often less than that of local sex workers, but a great deal more than they could command in Thailand (Skrobanek 1983). Initially, the destination of most Thai prostitutes was Western Europe. Some countries allowed Thai women to enter as performers at cultural events, with few visa requirements, provided that they returned home or went on to another country before renewing work contracts. Some of the women who went abroad at this time became agents, recruiting others into the sex trade overseas.

The success of these women attracted others to migrant work. Many low-skilled and poorly educated women saw in migration an opportunity to make money, but they were often ignorant of the nature of the work, and of the conditions in which they would be required to labour. Returnees were often less than candid when talking about their experiences abroad. Most admitted only to having worked in factories or in agricultural jobs, where the pay was good. (This reflects the world-wide experience of migration. People who leave find that they are obliged to keep up a pretence that they are happy and prosperous. This is the unwritten duty of those who depart to those who remain. When they come back, they must bring presents, and exude an air of success and achievement, even when the reality is far from this.) The relatively high earnings and remittances made the women who returned objects of admiration, regardless of whether family and friends were aware of the nature of their work (Massey et al. 1993).

There is evidence that sex tourism to Thailand played a part in the demand for Thai women in the entertainment/sex industry in foreign countries. They were popular with employers and customers alike in Europe, because they charged less than local women. In Germany in the early 1980s, Thai workers earned only 40–50 per cent of the average earnings of German sex workers. The rise in demand, and the opportunity to take advantage of Thai migrants in prostitution, encouraged agents to look further afield than the cities. Voluntary migration for sex work from the night clubs of Bangkok changed gradually into organised international trafficking in women.

This trafficking also includes 'mail order brides'. A woman who wants to migrate becomes the product of a bridal agency, which presents her with clients to choose from – and often to sample – before a deal is clinched. She then goes to the country of the foreigner as his wife

(Foundation for Women 1989). The promise of marriage to a wealthy foreigner – and all foreigners are perceived as such – allows the agent to attract poor women. She may find, however, that instead of marriage, she has been sold on to other agents and employers in her country of destination.

Factory workers and domestic helpers are also susceptible to exploitation. One such case was featured in local newspapers in August 1995, when 68 Thai garment workers, most of them women, were rescued from a sweatshop in Los Angeles. Contrary to what they had been told about conditions of work, they had been working a 16-hour day for less than US$1 an hour. In a closed compound, under armed guard, they had average 'debts' of US$4,800, incurred as travelling expenses (*Thai Rath* 5 August 1995).

Anti-Trafficking Laws

National anti-prostitution laws have been based on the 1949 UN Convention for the Suppression of Traffic in Persons and the Exploitation of Prostitution of Others. This reflects the emphasis on the trafficking for prostitution only. But the 1949 Convention has been overtaken by events, and does not take account of changing attitudes towards prostitutes and prostitution. The Convention calls for governments to eradicate prostitution, and to prosecute those involved, regardless of whether they undertake the work voluntarily or not. Prostitutes are to be rehabilitated, and laws regulating prostitution abolished. More positively, it does call for the provision of social services to those who have suffered as a result of trafficking, and for the control of employment agencies, both legal and illegal. The Convention also requires governments to assist and shelter those who need it while awaiting repatriation.

The 1979 Convention on the Elimination of All Forms of Discrimination Against Women (CEDAW) calls on governments to take all appropriate measures, including legislation, to suppress all forms of traffic in women and the exploitation of the prostitution of others (Article 6). The 1990 Convention on the Rights of the Child also demands that governments take all appropriate measures to prevent the traffic in children (Article 35). In 1928 there was a Royal Decree in Thailand on Trafficking of Women and Children, following the adoption of the 1921 International Convention on Trafficking of Women and Children. This decree contains a number of shortcomings, including the lack of a specific penalty for smuggling women and children out of the country. The penalty for traffickers – 1,000 baht – is absurdly low some 70 years later.

The Decree does not cover boys who are trafficked (Rayanakorn 1993; Skrobanek 1995).

Effectiveness of legal measures

In many countries, the traffic in human beings has been recognised as a crime in law, and international conventions have been ratified. But trafficking continues. Few countries provide reliable reports on the incidence of trafficking. It seems that both national laws and the 1949 Convention are ineffective in preventing the traffic in women. There are a number of reasons:

- Most law enforcement is practised against the victims rather than the traders and beneficiaries.
- There are difficulties in collecting evidence from the trafficked women, who fear that their illegal status as immigrants and/or prostitutes will lead to their imprisonment or deportation.
- Statements in court from prostitutes have carried less weight than evidence from defendants.
- The 1949 Convention adopts a moralistic position on the existence of prostitution and argues for its abolition. Regardless of such attitudes, abolition is almost certainly impossible. The international police force, Interpol, have said that governments will be unable to implement anti-trafficking legislation if trafficking remains tied to prostitution (Van der Vleuten 1991: 35).

5

Features of the Traffic in Women

Research by the Foundation for Women (FFW) among women migrant workers from both rural and urban areas of Thailand reveals patterns of migration. Studying these patterns shows how trafficking in women comes about. There are two types of migration of Thai women: two-step migration, where the woman worker moves first from her village to the city for employment, and from there travels overseas; and one-step migration, where the woman goes abroad directly from her village, usually to find employment or to marry a foreigner. There has also been migration and trafficking of women into Thailand, mostly from neighbouring countries. In some cases, foreigners have gone directly to villages to recruit sex workers. This chapter focuses on patterns of migration, and their impact on women. All names used in the examples in this and the following chapters are fictitious.

The Growth of Trafficking in Women: the View from the Village

In Thailand, prostitution was legal in the reign of King Rama V (1868–1910). Brothels were first legally registered in 1908, and most were run by Chinese men, although their clients were both Thai and Chinese. Apart from Thai women and girls, there were prostitutes from China, Japan and some Western countries (Metta-rikanondhu 1983: 30).

In the mid-19th century, Thailand opened its markets to international competition. This led to a gradual change from subsistence production to producing for the international market. The international trafficking of women and children accompanied the increase in the volume of trade between countries, particularly women who came to service Chinese labour migrants into the country.

In recent times, according to informants from villages in the north, trafficking in womem and children became a serious issue in the late 1960s. This included women and children forced to engage in prostitution, among whom the youngest were, reportedly, no more than twelve years old. In north-east Thailand, labour migration, both male and female, was established before this. Migration for commercial sex work rose significantly in the 1960s and 1970s, with the establishment of US military bases in Thailand and neighbouring countries. Pattaya, in particular, was developed as a tourist destination and centre for commercial sex, second only to the Patpong district in Bangkok. Most women who came to work in Patpong were not coerced into doing so.

It was found by the researchers that trafficking from the north of Thailand was more established and more systematic than from the north-east. This may be because general labour migration of both women and men was more prevalent from the north-east, and therefore trafficking to the city was both superfluous and less lucrative.

The history of migration for commercial sex work comprises three distinct periods.

Beginning, 1967–1977

The motive for migration was to overcome family poverty. Women who left had made a decision to improve the family's financial circumstances by working as prostitutes, or at other jobs – child-minding, or domestic help – in the cities. Some explanations of their reasons for becoming sex workers were given to researchers.

> Our family was poor, Mom and Dad were suffering. We wanted to help them by making the burden lighter. (Rim Mon village)

> I had no alternative in life. I was to go to work in the south. My family had suffered a lot through poverty. That's why my Mom sold me. I had to go because I loved them. (Soi Dao village)

> Nobody forced me to go into prostitution. I have never felt fed up. My parents could not afford to educate me. Commercial sex was my only option. In the old days, my family and I lived in a shack. My parents could not earn enough to keep all of us. Some days I had nothing to eat. I didn't even have a piece of land to live on. (Rim Mon village)

Through prostitution the young and poorly educated could help fulfil their families' needs. The primary destinations at that time were Bangkok and the south of Thailand.

There was negligible enforcement of anti-trafficking laws, and the number of young women moving overseas for sex work increased. An international network gradually came into existence, which included some of these early women migrants: they became recruiters and managers of sex workers. During this period, two-step migration dominated – from village to city, and thence to foreign countries.

Rural–urban migration has a long history. Only from the late 1960s did the sex industry become a major objective of migrants, and this coincided with the growth of known sex-tourism centres. The south of Thailand catered for clients mainly from Malaysia and Singapore. In Bangkok, foreign customers came primarily from Europe and the Arab states. The considerable earnings, and sometimes continuing financial support, from one or more foreign customers attracted other young women to join friends in the same business.

There have also been distinct patterns of movement between urban centres within the country, either to satisfy the brothel and bar owners, to stay ahead of the law, or to find better wages and conditions, as the sex industry expanded in some areas and contracted in others. Movement was common from the south to bars in Bangkok, and sometimes back again, according to seasonal fluctuations in the business.

The pioneers of international migration for prostitution were sex workers in Pattaya and Patpong who went to Europe. Others went to Malaysia and Singapore from the southern provinces. Some followed customers who assisted them with entry into their country. Some women migrants who went as domestic workers, particularly to Singapore and the Gulf, later worked in bars and brothels to supplement their income.

Germination, 1978–1987

Poverty continued to be the main factor impelling young women to migrate for prostitution, but other factors also appeared at this time. Some parents, seeing the daughters of other families return with considerable wealth, were induced to 'sell' their daughters. This provided them with a cash advance, to be paid off by their daughter's labour in the sex trade. Some of these transactions took place without the involvement of a broker.

From our case studies, it emerges that younger girls were engaging in prostitution during this time, and a simultaneous rise in the number of brokers was recorded. The debt of young women rose to reach sometimes twice as much as the sum given in advance. These advances varied from 3,000–7,000 baht (US$125–292). Our research in Rim Mon and Soi Dao showed direct routes to the sex outlets of Bangkok and the south. There are examples of girls who escaped from sex work into which they had been coerced, and who were returned to their captors, or 'sold' on elsewhere, to maintain the income of their families. Some sex workers were arrested and sent to a house of rehabilitation for one year, as specified in the 1960 Act for the Abatement of Prostitution. One year without income often left them more desperate for cash, and they returned to sex work. It is noteworthy that the trafficking of young women in this period was often supported and encouraged by their parents.

Other contributory factors included family illness and family debt. Northern girls, married at a young age to older men and abandoned, widowed or left without means of support also added to the pool of potential migrants.

During this same period there was an increase in the flow of migrant workers from the north-east to the countries of the Gulf and Singapore in particular. Information from Khon Na suggests that migrants were originally mostly male, but women began to follow their husbands and brothers. Many were domestic workers, not sex workers. This is quite different from the experience of the north. Some women were introduced to brokers with a view to contracting marriages abroad. Our research found that women from the north-east tended to enter into marriage with men from Taiwan, while those from the north were introduced to men from Singapore and Malaysia.

Growth, 1988–1996

This period is dominated by women migrating for prostitution. Pring, a woman from Soi Dao, described such migration thus:

> There are two types of prostitutes. The first type are spoiled teenagers, who want to have a car, a house, to be well-dressed with gold ornaments and lots of money to spend. And this is a new social status for them. The second type are women who are forced into prostitution by necessity, such as separation from husband, being widowed, the poverty of their parents, or debt.

In Soi Dao, we found that some of the girls in the sex industry were daughters of women who had previously done the same work. Prao, for example, was taken by her mother Pring to Telephone House, a sex venue in Sungaikolok. Auong, another second-generation sex worker, started her work in Bangkok, at a house with many other women from the same village. She later moved on to Pattaya.

Migration to Japan increased, and many women from the north-east assumed that this would follow a similar pattern to migration to the Gulf or Singapore, where they could choose between domestic and sex work.

Our research shows that agents' fees were often not revealed until their arrival in Japan, and that these were of the order of 20,000–40,000 baht (US$830–1,660).

Women going to Europe during this period were going chiefly from Pattaya and Bangkok, with the assistance of foreign customers. Some were deceived, and found themselves working as prostitutes in spite of the promises of their boyfriends. Our research in Pattaya found an informal information network among sex workers, which advised women about migration to Europe. The most vulnerable women are those of ethnic minority groups and women from neighbouring countries. Traffickers target them because they are ill-informed about the sex industry.

This period of growth in migration for prostitution includes the development of direct routes from villages to destinations overseas. There have been many reports of deception. One woman in Khon Na who went to Japan said:

> I was told it was a comfortable job, with good pay. It was in service at a restaurant. There was a lot of work available; you could choose what you wanted to do. There were many positions open for workers at the restaurant, and if you wanted it, the work was there. I was told I'd get the salary, as well as tips from the customers.

Many women do not understand what a service job is. They do not realise that 'service work' overseas usually means sex work. No one warns them that they may be subject to ill-treatment. Another woman in Khon Na said:

> The agent told me I could do the other job; there was no need to work in commercial sex service. But when I arrived I was sold like the others. It was made worse, because I worked without pay. I was to live in the countryside. I thought I could choose the job when I got there, but I was denied the right to do so. If I didn't work, I was ill-treated. If anybody told them lies, and it was found out, she was punished. And some were killed.

Despite reports of terrible experiences that come back to the village, many women are still willing to take the chance. Direct routes from villages to overseas destinations are expanding. Some agents are reported to have taken money from the woman's family on the strength of a promise of marriage to a foreigner. En route, some women have been forced to work as prostitutes before they reach their destination.

Information from Bangkok confirms that foreign women have recently been imported into Thailand for prostitution. During the Vietnam war, women from Hong Kong were said to have been employed in bars on Petchburi Road in Bangkok. Since the late 1980s, women from

Burma and China have been brought in and forced to work in the sex industry. It is suggested that Thai women are becoming more knowledgeable, and no longer use the services of recruiting agents to find work in the sex industry. Agents have therefore extended their activities to where cheaper and less assertive workers can be found.

The increase in the incidence of HIV infection has created a demand for younger women. We picked up reports that businessmen from Hong Kong were asking local agents for young virgins. Case studies show that young girls who are brought to the agent are on average between 14 and 19 years of age. Some cannot find work in bars because of their youth, so work is arranged through the agent.

Saeng, a 14-year-old girl from Burma, was sold by her elder sister for 2,000 baht (US$83). When she was taken to the brothel, she was refused, because of her age. The agent kept her at home to do domestic work. One day, the agent 'uncle' was drunk, and she feared she would be raped. She climbed over the fence and escaped.

A girl from the Akha hilltribe was sold for 2,000 baht when she was 10. She was later sold to a brothel in the south for 40,000 baht (US$1,600). She worked in the brothel for six years before being helped by the police.

It is also common that when women return to the village, they take up sex work again because of the potential earnings. For example, after Moei was taken home from a sex establishment, she realised she had no wish to return to work in the rice field, because the work was very hard. She preferred to go back to prostitution, and looked forward to finding a foreign customer for the sake of the financial support she could expect. There was also evidence in Rim Mon of foreign men visiting villages for sex. The local agent acted as middle-man between the villagers and the foreign clients. The women and girls involved were often former sex workers who had gone back home, while most clients were Japanese men. The arrangement was presented as a marriage-type relationship, with the payment of a dowry to the women's parents, and a monthly allowance to her. In some instances, clients provided money for housing and furniture.

Many women who have been in prostitution overseas have encouraged their relatives to develop relationships with foreigners. It was thought that by doing so, they would be helping the family's financial situation without having to go overseas.

Chan urged her two nieces to live with Japanese men, friends of her husband. The girls did not enjoy the experience. Chan reminded Bee, one of the nieces, why they should be patient: 'They give us hundreds of thousands. We must be patient and show we are worthy of that payment. Just stay with them until you have enough savings for a house; then you can leave them.' Bee's parents had been trying to control her by not allowing her to go out with friends, for fear that something bad would happen, and her Japanese 'husband' would cease supporting her. Bee regularly received 7,000 baht a month.

In these cases, the satisfaction of the man is paramount. If he is not satisfied he will leave. The women are in a very vulnerable position. Many customers believe that buying women directly from the village will protect them against the risk of HIV, as well as save them money, since costs in the village are lower than in the city.

In a village near Ton Yang, there was a report of a foreign tourist seeking a young wife without the mediation of a broker.

A foreign tourist rode a motorbike around the village in order to chat with the local women. He met Ms Dok Or on her way to the rice field. He accompanied her, and met her older and younger sisters there. He didn't like the older one, because she was fat, but took a fancy to the younger, who was only 15. The following day, he returned, chatted with Ging, and expressed his interest in her. He made her sit in his lap, which frightened her. She told him she was married.

He came back to the village, and went straight to the house of another young woman, Paungh. He said he would buy a farm and a house for Paungh's family. Finally, he asked her mother if he could marry her. Paungh's mother had no objection, but insisted on a wedding ceremony. The man agreed, and told Paungh he would stay with her three months a year. He gave her mother 3,000 baht to prepare food for the wedding party. Paungh's mother asked for more, but the man refused.

Conclusion

The trade in women in Thailand began with migration for work – voluntary or involuntary – in the sex industry. Our research shows that most women in the sex trade are young. The Penal Code and the Act for the Abatement of Prostitution contain safeguards for those under the age of 18, and more for those under 15. These laws are not rigorously enforced.

The early motivation for labour migration was the alleviation of poverty. More recently, women have been choosing migration for sex work because they have learned that a good income can be gained in this way. There is now greater awareness of what going overseas to work will entail. As the two-step migration pattern has moved into a one-step migration, we have also seen women coming into Thailand for sex work. It has been widely reported that impoverished women from Eastern Europe have been working in Patpong and Pattaya.

The change to one-step migration has meant that women leaving the country tend to be younger and less experienced than the early migrant sex workers. They are therefore less able to protect themselves from deception and abuse, and they rarely have the personal contacts to support them when things go wrong.

6

Routes and Networks

There are clear patterns in the migration of women from villages to cities and to foreign countries. Each pattern has its own routes and networks. Thailand has become an exporter of women migrants, a place of destination and a transit country. This chapter looks at these routes and networks, and their connection with migration for the sex industry at the national and international level.

The Routes

Data from the study indicate the following major pathways for prostitution:
*   from all regions to Patpong and Pattaya;
*   from the north to Suthisarn/Saphan Kwai;
*   from the north to the southern border with Malaysia;
*   from all regions to several European countries, Malaysia, Singapore, Japan, Taiwan and Hong Kong.

Domestic routes

To Patpong

> Tom, Tom, where you go last night?
> I love Muang Thai, I like Patpong.
> 'The girls are making Tom crazy.'
> I love Patpong, I love Muang Thai.
> Carabao

Loy was a girl from Roi-et in the north-east, who moved with her friends to work in a textile factory in Rangsit, just north of Bangkok. Her mother provided her with money for the bus ticket, which she was to pay back from her first month's salary. After working for some years, Loy became bored. She was angry with her family in Roi-et, because they kept asking her for money. Sometimes her mother came to the factory on pay-day to collect her pay-check. Loy began to think she would get nowhere if she carried on with her factory job. She switched to work as a masseuse at the Chao Praya Massage Parlour. There was a police sergeant whose part-time job was to urge customers to choose the girls on display in the glass window of the parlour. Every girl there had to be nice to this man. Loy was a fresh face and she slept with him. He was pleased with her, and directed many customers her way. Loy moved into a rented house with him, in an effort to save money. She changed jobs frequently and ended as a bar-tender in Patpong. She had many expenses. Dara, a Thai woman living in Germany, came looking for Thai women to work a three-month contract in Germany. Loy took the job, and came back well-off. She underwent cosmetic surgery to change her face, and went to and from Germany often, working as a prostitute. With the passage of time it became more difficult. Loy is now over 40, and still working in Patpong.

Patpong is a short, crowded thoroughfare in the heart of the business area of the capital. It is well known to tourists as a red-light area. It became an entertainment district during the Vietnam War. Go-go bars and sex shows brought more than 5,000 women from all over the country to work in the sex business.

> The first time Jieb sold sex to a foreigner in Patpong, she earned 10,000 baht with which she bought a rice-field for her mother. Ann came to Patpong to support herself through school when her family could no longer do so. Jad moved from working as a chicken cleaner to go-go dancing, and she introduced her sister to the work.

Most women who come to Patpong do so of their own free will. Others are coerced. At 14, Pum was forced by her lover to dance at a go-go bar in Patpong, and to give sexual services to customers in order to pay for his heroin addiction.

Patpong has become the destination of choice for women who enter prostitution, often in response to some financial crisis. Some women, like Loy, moved to Patpong after long experience of prostitution. Khaek, who now works in Patpong, married a Dutchman and worked as a prostitute while living with him in the Netherlands. Lily and Dara were pioneers in migrating to Europe, and they introduced others to the business. Now they are middle aged, and continue to work in Patpong. Most of the clients are foreign men, who have greater buying power than the average Thai. Women who work in Patpong feel superior to 'local prostitutes'. Working here opens up new opportunities, including the possibility of going abroad, marriage to a foreigner or sex work overseas.

Not all women come to Patpong with the intention of becoming sex workers. Ann was a waitress, but she became a prostitute under pressure from some customers. Mam wanted to work solely as a receptionist or bar-tender, but turned to sex work because there was a rule at the club where she worked that every employee must be available to customers for sex. By its nature, work in Patpong predisposed women to sell sex, sometimes in order to retain their jobs, but mostly to increase their income. Jobs in Patpong are not as independent as they may appear. Many conditions are imposed by club owners who want to maximise profit from their employees.

There is no clear-cut network or pathway bringing women to Patpong. Most hear about it from friends or relatives. No qualifications are required for working there, except being a young woman ready to sell sex. No one is refused. They are required to dress and dance provocatively, and some must perform in explicit sex shows. It is reported that there is a high use of tranquillisers and other drugs.

Most who work in Patpong began their careers as sex workers elsewhere. In some cases they were originally coerced into the business, but then chose to continue. Kob escaped from a prostitution chain in the south to work in a nude show in Patpong. Jad first sold sex to her uncle in return for a two-way ticket to Bangkok. She then persuaded her sister to work in Patpong for higher pay than she was then getting. Jad described her work thus:

> Compared to other labour, working in Patpong is much better, because we can dress up beautifully, we get more money to spend, and we are independent. No one treats us badly here. I choose this work because it does not require any previous experience. Even so, I don't like sex shows, because it is shameful in Thai society, and it is morally wrong.

Women in Patpong come from a wide range of family backgrounds, and have varying levels of education. Some did not finish elementary school, while others are currently enrolled on university courses. They earn money in Patpong to help them prepare for a better future. Pum summarised her Patpong experience:

> Patpong gives uneducated women the same chance to earn as educated ones. I will stay here because I want a lot of money. Even though there are risks, I think it's worth it. I'm not a virgin, so I have nothing to lose.

To Pattaya

Oh Pattaya, your moon is made of paper
Torn paper like torn dresses
People make their living in the market

Watch out for G.I.s, they are taking over the beach.
                                                Caravan

Noy is 33 and living in Pattaya with an Englishman. She left her village in
Roi-et with her sister who had worked in Pattaya before. Their gambling and
adulterous father was partly what impelled them to work in Pattaya. They
had been salesgirls at home but they needed money to support him. They
began as go-go girls in a bar. They had no intention of becoming sex workers,
but changed their minds because they wanted gold jewellery like other girls
there. Noy's sister went to live in Switzerland with her boyfriend, and she
sent money home. Noy will take her English boyfriend to visit her home in
Roi-et, in the hope he will build her a new house there.

Pattaya, a former fishing village, became a world-famous centre for sex
tourism during and after the Vietnam War. It became part of the tourist
package that men would be entertained by local Thai women. The
growth of Pattaya as a tourist resort attracted other women. But the real
wealth of Pattaya remains with the bar owners – mostly foreigners
married to Thai women.

The 26 women interviewed in Pattaya came from all over the country,
with the exception of the far south, although the Foundation for Women
has worked in Pattaya with women from this area. The largest group
came from Udon Thani (north-east), which had previously hosted an
American army base. One woman had come from the far north to do
cleaning work, but she had finished up as a bar girl. Their ages ranged
from 16 to 40. Of the 26, only four had never been married.

The routes to Pattaya are as open as those leading to Patpong. Many
spoke of poverty as a primary reason for taking this road. At home, they
work for low wages – about 60 baht (US$2.50) a day. They wanted
money to make a new life, a new home, to buy tools or a tractor to work
the rice-field. Many spoke bitterly of their family life. Some were beaten
by husbands, and said they were sick and tired of irresponsible men.

My man always used to beat me when he was drunk. He liked to have fun
with his friends, and was always out. He never gave me any money, so I ran
away to my mother who promised to put me through school. But my
grandmother said there was no money, and it was better for me to look for
work in Pattaya.

My man beat me up all the time, even when I was pregnant. He was always
jealous. His family looked down on me, so I left him. I really love my
children, so I came here to work for the sake of them and their future.

At first I came to work here because I wanted to show my husband I could
start a new life. I've never wanted to go back. I like it more every day. I want
money.

Many of the women were persuaded to come to Pattaya by female relatives or friends already working there.

> I broke up with my boyfriend and went home to my parents. My sister felt sorry for me, so she brought me here. She didn't tell me what the job was, because our parents would not have liked the idea. She told me to think about it carefully, because there was nothing for me at home.

> My friend told me not to commit suicide but to work for the money to send home instead. Before, I used to think bar girls were bad, but now I've become one myself.

One woman had asked her husband's permission to work in Pattaya so she could have gold jewellery like her friends. She used to hate foreigners and look down on prostitutes. She and her husband were very poor. She went to work as a dancer in a go-go bar, but was not a prostitute. Another woman said she was lured and sold by an acquaintance from her home village. Yet another was brought to work in a hotel to pay off her mother's debts. Most of the women who had come to Pattaya as sex workers spoke positively about their experience.

> If I had known about foreigners and Pattaya, I would have come here when I was 15 or 16. I would have worked hard and become very rich. I would not have married a Thai and had children. But I was too old when I came here.

Many of the women had been working as agricultural labourers, workers in food shops or cleaning women in hotels. Most came to Pattaya knowing they would sell sex.

> Once we get to Pattaya we are no longer decent. My sister said there is good money here for washing dishes. In fact, there is nothing like that. We have to dance in go-go bars. We can't go back home for fear of losing face. People know the only thing we have to sell in Pattaya is our bodies. We want to find other jobs, but we are uneducated. Academic degrees are needed for good jobs.

Unskilled and uneducated women have limited choices in the job market. If they work in restaurants or hotels in their home province they are often pressured to have sex with customers. In Pattaya, most customers are foreign.

> They told me I had to go out with a foreigner or I wouldn't get the bonus. I said I didn't want the bonus but they introduced me to foreigners anyway. They said that way I would have a bright future.

The money that can be earned in Pattaya leads many women to recruit their relatives and friends. Duan has two sisters working in Pattaya. One sister married an Australian, the other a Dutchman.

Besides go-go dancing and sex services in the bars, some Pattaya women work from brothels. Here, they are less independent; their freedom of movement outside the brothel may be restricted. Some work to pay off a debt to the owner. Their customers are mainly foreigners. Women in Pattaya are often persuaded to go abroad. Min worked in a bar and was convinced by a German businessman in Pattaya to go to Hong Kong. He did not tell her about the conditions of work: some women had to sleep with many men a night for low pay. They had no right to refuse.

> I never had so many customers – up to thirteen men a night. No one had told me about this. I cried. On the ninth day I was sent home by the police.

Even if the woman agrees to migrate for prostitution, the deception and subsequent exploitation cancel any free choice she may have made. Some women migrate to foreign countries in order to continue a relationship with a boyfriend. Of the 26 interviewed in Pattaya, five had been abroad with boyfriends, and a further seven hoped to go. Others had arranged to go for domestic work, with the help of foreign customers.

The information network in Pattaya appears to operate effectively. The women have also heard media reports of prostitution rings in other countries. Ned went to Norway to be a domestic servant, but will not repeat the experience.

> I don't want to go abroad because I'm afraid I'll be sold. I went to Norway because I knew a Thai there. I was told they take away your passport and put you in a whorehouse in Germany. There is nothing good there, only bad experiences.

To Suthisarn/Saphan Kwai

> Eay went to work in Suthisarn when she was 17. Her family was very poor. The roof of their house had collapsed. Her father borrowed money to buy a buffalo to work in the field, but it died. He fell deeply into debt. Eay sold her virginity for 5,000 baht. She worked for two months to pay back her father's debt.

Suthisarn is a street in the Saphan Kwai district of Bangkok. It has been a red-light district since the late 1960s, catering mainly to Thai men. The women are young and poor, and come mostly from the north. Suthisarn was one of the earliest sex work destinations for women migrating to Bangkok. Local agents were instrumental in this, and often accompanied the women from their home to Suthisarn. In Rim Mon, researchers were told that some agents were distinguished members of the community.

Each brothel employs between 20 and 30 women. Agents ask the brothel owners how many women they need, and then go to the villages to find them. They may approach a young woman directly, or speak to her parents first. Parents or guardians accompany the very young girls, since they have to meet the brothel owner personally, and agree to their children being employed there. Thinakorn, the agent from Rim Mon, said:

> We must bring the father or mother, or we will be accused of kidnapping the girl. The parents have to make an agreement with the brothel to get the advance payment.

This advance payment is generally between 5,000 and 30,000 baht (US$208–1,250). The debt will be paid back by the daughter, and will amount to twice the original sum. Some agents demand commission of 2,000 baht. Thinakorn says he pays for nothing. Travelling expenses and food are paid by the brothel owner. Agents like Thinakorn have a close relationship with the owners, and are well looked after by them. Thinakorn told us he had persuaded his wife's sister to go to Suthisarn. With the increasing numbers of women leaving the village for sex work, this ceases to be anything out of the ordinary.

Customers in Suthisarn are now both Thai and foreign. The foreigners are mostly from the Gulf and Japan. There were ten girls from Rim Mon who had received continuing financial support from customers they met in Suthisarn. Their patrons were all tourists from the Middle East, who made it a condition of their support that the women return to the village. These men visited once or twice a year. Some took the women on a visit to their country.

Apart from the established red-light districts, there are local massage parlours, brothels and restaurants in Bangkok where sex can be bought. Some girls are brought by agents directly to these places from the railway or bus stations. Others are accompanied by agents from their villages. Nuj was persuaded by an agent called Jampa to move to Bangkok. She worked in a big massage parlour for three years under close supervision, and was paid only 50 baht (US$2) a day. Jampa and her partner, Yonyuth, travel to the north to recruit women three times a month.

There were reports of serious violence associated with recruitment for and employment in these brothels.

> Pai was beaten by three men until she lost consciousness. She was sold to a brothel and forced to sleep with numerous customers each night. She was

sold on twice to brothels in other provinces. Pai worked without pay, and was provided with two meals a day. If she refused to work, she was beaten. She was too frightened to attempt an escape. She became pregnant, and was made to have an abortion. She is now sick with an AIDS-related illness.

In Soi Dao village, we heard of an agent called Sai Buo who specialises in procuring customers for young women who do not wish to work regularly as prostitutes, but only at times of financial crisis. Sai Buo takes a share of the money, and provides a room for the girl and the client. If the girl is a virgin, she can make a considerable amount of money.

To the south

Orn was 14 when, at her mother's insistence, she married a 28-year-old. He worked in a tobacco factory. He was very jealous, and frequently beat her. Orn endured it for seven years, and had two children before she left him. Not long after, her mother took her to Hat Yai. She obeyed her mother because of her love for her, and because she was poor. She also worried about her children. Her mother took a cash advance of 10,000 baht (US$416). Orn was required to pay back 20,000 baht. She worked in a masssage-parlour, as a three-star masseuse, and tried to send home 20,000–30,000 a month. Her mother often called or visited to ask for more money. Orn continued to obey her mother, for fear that she would abandon the children.

Pring went to Hat Yai, later to Malaysia and Singapore. She sent money to her parents in the village, who looked after her daughter, Prao. When Prao was at secondary school, the boys teased her as the daughter of a prostitute, and she felt angry. She wanted to become rich to protect herself against such criticism. She left school and told her mother she wanted to become a sex worker. Pring took her daughter to Singaikolok, signed a contract with a brothel, and received a 10,000 baht advance. Prao was 14 years old. Soon after she started work, there was a government crackdown on child prostitution, and Prao was sent home by the brothel keeper, who feared arrest.

Hat Yai and Singaikolok are near the border with Malaysia. The direct route from villages in the north to brothels in the south began in the late 1960s, and still continues. Two well-known recruiters for the southern brothels are local women, Ya Jai and Babieng. They had themselves worked in the south previously. Ya Jai had served a prison sentence for recruiting. Another local woman, Pen, operates her own call-girl business in Hat Yai.

The pattern of recruitment and employment is similar to that in Suthisarn, whereby the parents are expected to travel with under-age girls to sign a contract with the brothel owner. Travel costs are paid by the owner, but we heard of one agent, Yai, who charged the parents or young woman a service fee of 3,000 baht (US$125). Wan was persuaded by her aunt to migrate south when she was just 13. Her mother was paid 6,000 baht. Kob's mother received 3,000 baht from a Thai dance bar. Kob was a performer in sex shows, and she later moved to Bangkok. The researchers heard of a young Burmese woman, Sya, who was sold when she was 10 for 40,000 baht. The employers let her work as a waitress for two years before initiating her into prostitution. She said in her place of work there were a hundred young women from hill tribes, and they were often ill-treated. Some were locked in their rooms. One group of these young women escaped, but they were caught and beaten.

It was our impression, overall, that the young women from Rim Mon and Soi Dao were treated less cruelly. This helps to explain why the girls are willing to go, and why relatives encourage them to do so. Pring described the hierarchy of preferences of the customers: the most desirable girls are from the north, second from Burma, third from Vietnam, and lastly from the north-east. Kampo from Rim Mon described the foreign customers:

> These men are tired after their work so they come to have fun in Hat Yai where there are lots of girls. Thais are nice people, so they feel good here. There are girls in their own countries, but Thai women try to please them. Some customers persuaded the girls to go and work in Malaysia and Singapore. Some supported or married Thai women.

Nong, from Soi Dao, had one child with a Singaporean. In Rim Mon, there were three women who had left prostitution because they were supported by men from Singapore. One of these women works as a labour recruiter, mostly for men to work in Singapore.

To other urban centres

> Nung left school at third grade because she was mature and other children made fun of her. Her father was a drug addict and a gambler, who had sold their land to pay his debts. Nung's relatives came to visit, and they took her to Aranyaprathet, near the border with Cambodia. Nung helped with housework. In the house were many girls. After five months, her relative told her to dress up, and took her to the district fair, where she was introduced to a prominent businessman. He said Nung was cute and obedient, and he thought of her as a daughter. He took her home. She woke that night to find him taking off her clothes. She tried to fight him off, but he hit her till she lost consciousness; and then he raped her. She was forced to work in the brothel owned by this man, and she discovered that her relatives were working for him as recruiters. She worked for three years before moving on to a bar in Lopburi.

We found evidence of young women being taken to Rayong, Chonburi, Kanchanaburi, Aranyaprathet and Samutsakorn for prostitution. Most said they had been coerced or lured into the work. They then move on to bigger centres of the sex industry, but rarely return to the smaller towns. Conditions in these brothels appear to be more severe and the financial rewards inferior. This partly explains the tendency of brothel owners to keep tighter control over the women to prevent them from leaving.

International routes

Migration abroad for prostitution increased significantly in the late 1960s. At that time, most women made for Europe. Later, Malaysia, Singapore and Japan became major destinations. There is also evidence that women have migrated to the US, Australia, New Zealand and South Africa.

To Europe

Lily is from Hong Kong, and came to work in the Petchburi Road area during the Vietnam War. She married the owner of the bar so that she could remain legally in Thailand. She earned a reputation as a talented exotic dancer, and she taught this art to Thai women. She later married an American soldier, who was later based in Germany, and they got involved in the drug scene in Europe. She took up exotic dancing there to pay for their habit. She was imprisoned for drug possession and repatriated to Thailand.

Dara met Lily in Hamburg. She was born in Korat in the north-east. She left school after six years and worked as a domestic servant for a German couple, who were living temporarily in Korat as consultants on a dam project. Dara went with them back to Germany. When she arrived, they confiscated her passport, and she was forbidden to leave the house on her own. She was 16. She was forced to have sex with the man. When he went to Africa on business, the woman took Dara to a bar in the red-light district of Hamburg, and 'sold' her to the owner.

Lily and Dara became friends in the bar. The owner arranged her marriage to a German, so that she could stay in the country. Dara became involved in the drug scene, but returned to Thailand to avoid arrest. When her family learned of the work she had been doing, they treated her badly. Dara then became a recruiter, encouraging women from Patpong to work in bars in Germany.

Lily and Dara were early migrants to Europe, and their stories show how patterns of migration are perpetuated by means of the contacts and knowledge of experienced migrant sex workers. Dara recruited Loy, a bar-tender in Patpong, for a three-month contract in Germany. Loy voluntarily paid Dara a commission of 10,000 baht (US$416). Loy voluntarily travelled to and from Germany, and bought a car and a house with her earnings.

According to workers at Ban Ying in Berlin, a shelter for migrant women, visa restrictions imposed in 1991 did little to slow down the flow of sex workers into Germany, but it did increase their debt to agents. They reported that this debt now averages between DM10,000 and DM40,000 (US$7,500–30,000) (Ban Ying 1994).

> Su worked as a prostitute in several European countries. Her first visit was arranged with an agent who promised her a job as a waitress in Germany. She and another woman travelled there via Poland. A second agent handed them a letter at the border to give to the immigration officials. This stated they were political activists in Thailand, under threat of persecution, and requested political asylum. They were granted temporary residence. During this time, they paid their 200,000-baht debts by doing sex work. They were sent back to Thailand.

The networks between Thailand and Europe include former migrants and regular tourists to Thailand, all of whom get a commission from the transaction.

> Noy agreed to go with Sumontha to Europe on the promise of marriage to a foreigner. Sumontha was married to a Dane. She took 50,000 baht (US$2,080) from Noy's father and went with Noy to Europe. Sumontha then demanded 50,000 baht from the man who wanted to marry Noy.

To Malaysia and Singapore

Migrating to Malaysia and Singapore became popular only in the late 1980s. These countries have also been used as transit points for women *en route* to Japan, Taiwan and Australia.

> Nak went to Singapore twice before she married a man from her village in the north. She stopped sex work but became an agent for a network which included brothels in Hat Yai and Singapore. She charged each girl a commission of 7,000 baht (US$292).

> Hia Piew lived in Hat Yai and, like Nak, he worked for a network that extended to Singapore. He would approach women working in Hat Yai with a promise of opportunities to make 5,000 baht a day (US$208) in Singapore. Each woman was expected to pay him 30,000 baht for travelling and visa expenses, which he took on instalments at the rate of 1,000 baht a day. Only when the full amount was paid would he make the travel arrangements.

Tour companies form part of the network. The women pay the company for arranging passports, for loans to convince border officials that they have the means to support themselves, and for a guide to accompany them. The usual length of stay in Singapore is only 15 days, so they have to work hard to show any profit. They are under constant threat of arrest. Customers include Thai labourers as well as local Chinese.

Some women have walked into Malaysia, crossing the border in remote jungle areas. Some have entered Singapore by boat, following a circuitous route via Indonesia. The Malaysian authorities recorded 9,074 illegal Thai migrants in 1993, according to an interview with a Malaysian police officer. The authorities find it harder to arrest the agents, because they are better at concealment. An official at the Thai Embassy in Kuala Lumpur spoke of reports that Thai-speaking Chinese Malays were buying village children of 15–16 from their parents, on payment of 20,000 baht. They married the girls, but on their return to Malaysia, they destroyed the marriage licences and resold the children.

To Hong Kong and Taiwan

> Lon is from Khon Na. She went to Taiwan on the advice of an agent, to whom she paid a fee of 40,000 baht (US$1,660). He told her, 'It's better to do domestic work in Taiwan because your employer may marry you.' Lon did marry her Taiwanese. She was 22.

One of the most vulnerable groups of migrants to foreign countries are those without Thai citizenship, those who, despite long residency in the country, are not recognised by the government as Thai citizens. Thai embassy officials resist requests for help to individuals who have no official citizenship status.

Besides Thai agents, foreign men are also involved in the networks. Min was accompanied to Hong Kong by a German, resident in Pattaya, who returned to Thailand after delivering her to an employer. She was arrested nine days later, and sent back to Bangkok.

> I don't want to see that German again because he was not good to me. I only know the system of working in Pattaya. In Hong Kong, if I didn't accept a lot of customers I was scolded. The lodgings were dirty.

There were reports that women working in the Hong Kong bars received only about 10 per cent of the money that changed hands, the rest going to the bar owner, the hotel and the escort. This, and the poor working conditions, made Hong Kong a less popular destination for migrant sex workers. In 1994, however, when Japan imposed new restrictions on 'entertainers' visas', and it became harder for women to enter the country, Hong Kong gained in popularity. Some women, believing they were going to Japan, were taken to Hong Kong instead (*Thai Rath* 25 July 1995).

To Japan

Paeng, following the advice of Sam-ang, daughter of the village headman, went from Ton Yang village to Japan when she was 16. Paeng's parents were in debt because her father's labour migration to the Gulf had failed. Paeng travelled on false documents and worked in a restaurant. She soon found a Japanese boyfriend, and paid off her debt. She bought the passport of another Thai woman for 40,000 baht, and returned to Thailand. She stayed long enough to get her own passport. She re-entered Japan, working hard enough to set up a recruitment/employment network of her own. With the money she sent home, her parents bought land, a house and a car. As a result of her success, there were many eager recruits for work in Japan among the young women of Ton Yang.

Japan has been a major migration route for sex work. Meay, a big-time agent, said, 'During the boom, we had to charter the whole plane to carry all the women' (Chivit Ton Suu 1994). The networks included organised criminal gangs in Japan and Thai officials. Of the latter, Meay said, 'Some days they issued hundreds of passports'. Women working in bars and massage parlours that catered for Japanese men in Bangkok were the most likely to travel to Japan for sex work. There was very little cross-over between the groups which went to Europe and those which went to Japan.

Saeng-Deuan was the first woman from Rim Mon to go to Japan. She had previously worked in Hat Yai, Bangkok and Singapore. She made her first trip to Japan in the late 1970s. On her return to the village, she became a local agent, encouraging younger women to agree to marriage-type arrangements with Japanese men.

The Japanese route has become increasingly prominent since the mid-1980s. It is estimated that at present there are between 80,000 and 100,000 Thai women sex workers in Japan. There have been numerous reports of ill-treatment, imprisonment and serious physical abuse. Instances of deceit involving very young women are commonplace. The researchers heard of Vi, who at 14 left for Japan as a domestic servant. On arrival, she was 'sold' to an employer, and told she had to work off her debt of 600,000 baht (US$25,000).

Throughout all the transactions involved in the trade, the woman's debt increases dramatically. The agent's fee is in the order of 15,000–30,000 baht (US$625–1,250). When they are 'sold' to employers in Japan, this amount is added to the 'bond' which they must also pay back, usually at more than double the agreed price. For example, reports came of Japanese employers paying the agent 200,000 baht for the services of a woman when she arrived in Japan, but her debt was inflated to between 400,000 and 700,000 baht. This is bonded labour. There were further examples of women being 're-sold' before their first debt was paid off, and being bound a second time, with a proportionate increase in debt. It can take sex workers a year to pay off debts of this magnitude.

> Sam-ang is a recruiting agent in Ton Yang, in league with a Bangkok-based agent. As part of her payment, she gets a free trip to Japan each year. Over five years, she has persuaded 14 young women to work in Japan. She tells them, 'There are lots of jobs in Japan, but if you want to make big money, you have to do service work to get tips from the customers'.

> Dokmai left Japan before paying off her debt. 'The agent said we could do other jobs besides sex. But when I got there, I was bought just like the other women. I didn't get paid for much of the work, and I had to live up country. I thought I could choose the work, but I couldn't. If we didn't work we were punished. Some women were killed.'

Women without passports of their own are provided with false documents. They may have to pass through other countries in order to hide their traces and origins. Sorn, from Khon Na, went to Malaysia *en route* to Japan, collecting a Malaysian woman and child on the way, so that they looked like a family group on holiday. Some have been escorted by Thai or foreign men posing as their husbands. Nung said she had to remain with her escort for two weeks, going from city to city until they found a 'buyer'. Finally, two women, one Japanese, the other Taiwanese, shared the cost, and bought her for 200,000 baht. Nung had to pay back 400,000 baht. Some experienced Thai women move into buying the new women as they fly in, and then approaching restaurant owners. They have usually established their connections thoroughly beforehand.

This trade is profitable enough to continue to attract new agents, buyers and women willing to go abroad for sex work, despite all the risks. The number of women going to Japan seems to be susceptible to swings in the inflation rate there, and periodic clampdowns on illegal immigrants. There were reports of Japanese agents selling women on to other countries.

Other routes

The USA, Australia, New Zealand, Canada and China also receive migrant Thai women as sex workers, although in smaller numbers than the principal countries. Thailand is now also receiving women from neighbouring countries, some of whom remain in Thailand, while others move on to third countries. There is considerable documented evidence of Burmese women being trafficked across the Thai border into brothels. In Ranong province, bordering the south of Burma, there are some 40 brothels, each reportedly employing around 100 women. Women from

Yunnan province in China are also being brought in for prostitution in Bangkok, Chiang Rai in the north and Singaikolok in the south. These women have mentioned the involvement of border police, who take about 3,000 baht (US$125) for each woman allowed to pass.

Most recently there have been reports of women sex workers in Bangkok from Eastern Europe. One account spoke of seven young women from Romania, who had been hired to do a cabaret act in Bangkok, but who had been coerced into prostitution by their Turkish agent.

Networks and Agents

Networks are the channels whereby women are transported along the routes that lead from home to the red-light districts in Thailand or overseas. The agents employed along each route are either employees of companies or they work for themselves, individually or as part of a team. For the purpose of our research, we divided agents into four groups:

Type A

Type A agents are usually local people, often either influential community leaders or women who have themselves already experienced migration for sex work.

> Jampa and Yongyuth operate in the Mae Sai area among local hill tribes, recruiting for massage parlours in Bangkok. Jampa herself is a former prostitute, and Yongyuth was a pimp. They recruit under-age girls like Nuj (see pp. 1–3), who was only 15 when she went to work for a massage parlour which was strictly controlled.

> Sai Buo works as an agent, mostly in Chang Pheuk village. She has a house in Bangkok for village girls who want to sell their virginity for one-off large sums, or to work irregularly in the sex industry. She provides both lodgings and customers. At Songkran (Thai traditional New Year celebrations in April), Sai Buo hosts a ceremony in Bangkok in aid of the temple of Chang Pheuk.

> Babieng lives in a village near Chang Pheuk, and recruits women for prostitution in the south. Babieng uses his local knowledge to advantage. He approached Pring when her mother was seriously ill and their rice-field had just been mortgaged.

> Nai Yai, a local leader of Rim Mon, is an agent who has contacts all over the country. He operates carefully, and makes sure the parents and girls are aware of the nature of the work they will undertake. Under-age girls must be accompanied by a parent or guardian to their new place of work.

Thinakorn, also a villager in Rim Mon, is 38, and holds a degree in Religious Studies. An experienced migrant labourer, he is active in local community activities and services. He recruits for the Suthisarn/Sapahn Kwai district.

Nang Pen of Rim Mon is 36, and has her own call-girl business in Hat Yai. At 22, she went south to work in the sex industry. She is well respected and admired in the village.

Nang Huan, also of Rim Mon, has two daughters in sex work in Bangkok. Huan now recruits other young women.

Type B

This type of agent works for an employment agency and is well-known among night-club and bar owners. Company offices are located close to main bus and railway stations, especially the central stations in Bangkok. They send girls to work in night-clubs and bars. These employment agencies usually take the first three months' wages as commission. Our research also found evidence of people employed by the night-clubs going directly to the stations to approach the women as they arrive.

Type C

These agents send Thai women to work abroad. Some are themselves experienced migrant sex workers. Each route has its own agents.

Sumontha's home town is near Ton Yang, but she spends most of her time in Denmark with her Danish husband. When she visits the village, parents pay her 50,000 baht to arrange migration to Europe for their daughters.

Wilaiwan is an officer of the Forestry Department. She recruits for a network based in Germany, who post her a commission once the woman has arrived.

Nak, of Rim Mon, used to work in Singapore. For 7,000 baht, she arranged transport to and contacts in Singapore.

Poonsap, of Ton Yang, worked in Singapore for 10 years and married a Singaporean. After visits home, she takes young women back with her to Singapore. One of these, Saisamorn, died a few years ago, apparently of an AIDS-related illness.

Saeng-Deuan of Rim Mon, and her Japanese husband, recruit women for Japanese men to visit in the village. 'We don't want our children to go far away, because we don't know the foreigners. When they stay at home like this, we don't have to work hard, but we still receive an income. If we save, we can soon build a house. We won't have to suffer. I want all those who are like sisters and relatives to me to be happy. The foreigners are easy. They don't stay long or come too often. Husbands we choose for ourselves are not as nice as this. To marry a man from the village is to suffer. This way, we don't get tired and we don't have to worry. We only want money. What's more, if we go into prostitution, we're at risk from disease. I don't think what we do is prostitution. We think of the men as our husbands. It's like having a husband who works abroad to send us money. We are faithful to them, and don't go with other men. They are happy to support us. We're like their wives.'

Puang-panga of Chang Pheuk village operates a long-distance telephone service. She is a middle person, who supplies the women needed by a Bangkok agent for travel to Japan. She charges the Bangkok company between 2,000 and 5,000 baht per recruit.

Nai Thong lives in a village near Ton Yang. He sends groups of 10 at a time by van to Bangkok, where false travel documents are provided for the journey to Japan.

Nang Petch lives in Nong Kai near Ton Yang. She informs women of the nature of the work they can expect in Japan, but she does not tell them about the huge debt they will incur. Her sister has also joined her in recruiting.

Nai Sakchai, an official at the Labour Office of Nong Khai province, said, 'Work in Thailand commands a salary of only a few thousand baht. It's better to work in Japan and come home rich.' He sent two women to Japan to work as prostitutes.

Nang Huan once arranged for a group of 10 women to leave from Na Thong for Japan. Each made a down payment of 25,000 baht. They waited in a flat in Bangkok for travel documents, and she arranged plastic surgery for those who wanted it. She also organised customers while they waited. Nang Huang went with them to Japan. She confiscated their passports, and resold them at 15,000 baht each to women there who wanted to return to Thailand.

Besides individual agents, we found evidence of teams of five and six, each headed by a boss. The team lets women in Patpong know that they can be taken to Japan for only 10,000 baht. The boss usually goes with them, and negotiates the 'sale' price.

Type D

This type of agent works for a company with good connections in particular countries or regions.

The Bangkok-based Dara Songsaeng company is owned by a husband-and-wife team. They send women to Germany on the understanding that they will work as waitresses for a daily wage of 10,000 baht and free accommodation. The company advances money to cover all costs. The women are flown to Poland, and then cross the border into Germany. Turks and Germans meet them and deliver them to brothels in Berlin.

Khru Dok Khae company sends women to Japan. When the women apply, they must spend a month or two in Bangkok, getting ready for the journey. During this time, marriages to foreigners may be arranged, to facilitate entry into Japan.

Ngern Yen company operates out of Bangkok, trading with Japan. The waiting time is about a month, and the cost 30,000 baht. The women usually travel in groups of eight or ten.

Women in the Networks

Women who have previously been migrant sex workers have a significant role in the networks that send and employ new recruits. Their relationship is both direct, as agents, and indirect, in that they provide role-models for the younger women. There are also women who provide help to migrant women when they get into trouble.

Si came from Ton Yang, but now lives in Japan with her Japanese husband. She was a sex worker when she met him. She maintains contact with other Thai women working in bars. Si helped two pregnant women who had run away from their club before their debts were paid off. She advised them to go to the police, and they were sent back to Thailand. Si's house is now a meeting-place for Thai women.

Paeng and Peaun offer assistance, but always profit from their interventions. They will pay off a woman's debt to help her escape from an employer who is ill-treating her, but only on condition that the woman works for them to reimburse a highly inflated debt. Once such woman was Jan Raem, whose pimp husband was treating her badly. Paeng asked her boyfriend, a member of the Yakuza (Japanese mafia) to rescue Jan Raem and to conceal her in a village for a while. Jan Raem then had to work in a restaurant to pay back a debt of 400,000 baht to Paeng. Paeng and Peaun also act as local money-lenders.

Conclusion

The process of migration for prostitution begins with the woman's decision to migrate, sometimes knowing the nature of the work, sometimes not. The networks that make possible and profit from this form of migration extend from the local village to distant foreign cities, and they draw upon women and men of widely different backgrounds.

Local level: Parents and other relatives play an important role in the decision to migrate in search of work, either directly, by negotiating contracts themselves, or indirectly, through the expectation that daughters will provide for their parents. Local agents are sometimes influential community leaders, or they may be newly rich returning migrants; more rarely, they will be foreign visitors.

*Provincial level:*Agents at this level act as go-betweens for local agents and city employers or networks. Some have worked abroad, and are familiar with the routes. Their income may come from commission paid by the family or the woman, and from employers or agents in the city.

National level: Agents in Bangkok are the key to migration. They help prepare the women by offering a range of beauty treatments, teaching them certain skills, arranging travel documents, planning the route and providing escorts to accompany the women and to conceal their reason for entering the country in question.

International level: International agents buy from national agents, and re-sell women to night-club and bar owners. Sometimes the networks extend beyond their country of residence. They may also travel to Thailand to choose the women themselves.

The profits to be made are high. The route to Japan, for example, requires an initial outlay of 20,000–30,000 baht (US$830–1,250), to be paid by the woman or her family. By the time she reaches Japan, the money which changes hands may be ten times as much. Her final debt may reach 700,000 baht. Risks are relatively low compared to other forms of illegal trade – such as drugs or arms – partly because of the collusion of the trafficked woman.

The results of the research, especially in Ton Yang and Khon Na in the north-east, point to a link between the export of labour in general and the trade in women. Women began to migrate in the company of husbands or male relatives. Labour-exporting agencies were quick to grasp the potential of this movement and began to advertise directly for women, sometimes using deceit (Archavanitkul 1993). In some cases, a consequence of labour migration of male relatives was an even greater family debt, which forced other members of the family – women – to seek opportunities for high earnings away from their villages.

Strategies to address this trade must consider policies on both the export of labour and on tourism, as well as the extensive networks that cross national boundaries. Relative poverty in the rural areas and among women are also inseparable from the issue. Any proposals for eradicating the trade in women must address the structural as well as the individual elements that give rise to it.

7

Working Conditions

It is clear that women who enter the sex industry often do so in order to improve the economic situation of themselves and their families. In some places of work they are subject to major exploitation. They are often treated as goods to be sold and traded between sex establishments. This chapter examines the position of women in the venues where they work.

Data from the Ministry of Public Health identifies more than 24 types of sex establishment. Our research confirmed the wide range of places where sex is bought and sold. The circumstances in which this takes place are equally varied for the women, from forced prostitution to independent soliciting in bars.

Sex Establishments in Thailand

Closed brothels

Our research found that women taken to closed brothels are usually young, often from minority groups, or illegal immigrants from neighbouring countries. Many move on to independent sex work. Closed brothels exist all over the country. The charge to customers is relatively low, and they are patronised by local men and travellers alike. Many brothels have strict rules which severely limit the freedom of the workers. The woman's bedroom is often used for servicing clients. One closed brothel had a concealed room, covered with a wooden board, which was unlocked to bring out the woman in order to entertain the customer. Women are often unpaid, since their earnings go directly to the owner to pay off the debt she or her family has incurred in the initial advance.

There can be many clients in one night. The fee paid by the client is 60–150 baht (US$2.50–6.25). Brothels house between 30 and 60 workers.

Table 7.1: Sex trade establishments in Thailand, 1994

Type of Business	No.
brothel	1,372
hotel	200
night-club	80
beer bar	598
ram wong bar (traditional dance)	6
go-go bar	136
discotheque	12
restaurant	1,887
coffee shop	30
cafe	257
cocktail lounge	73
pub	73
tea house	30
massage parlour	154
traditional massage parlour	309
beauty salon	11
barber	45
escort/call-girl agency	22
gay bar	67
guest-house	3
karaoke bar	322
sauna	8
bungalow	23
others	36
Total	5,754

Source: Venereal Disease Division, Department of Disease Control, Ministry of Public Health.

The study found that some brothels prefer to buy very young women and wait a few years before introducing them to prostitution. The girl may be raped by the owner or sold to a customer for 5,000–8,000 baht

(US$208–330). Some women have been 'broken in' several times, with the price varying according to age. The only money she may earn during the period of bonded labour is from tips given by customers over and above the fee. Some women have been sold off to a second brothel when their debt at the first one is paid off. We heard of one woman who had been sold to three brothels. She was released to have an abortion, only to be informed by the doctor that she was HIV-positive.

Health care is minimal, and the rate of sexually transmitted diseases high. The risk of HIV infection from customers is constant. The response of the owners seems to be that workers are easily replaced, so the provision of safe working conditions is not a priority. There were reports of women who had escaped, sometimes with the help of a client. There were also stories of failed attempts, and of women severely punished as an example to others.

Open brothels

The open brothel may be a house or a hotel. Women working in such places are semi-independent. They can go out shopping alone or with a chaperone, although some brothels discourage going out. There were reports of women refused permission to contact their home or to read letters they had received. In the open brothels, certain rules must be observed:

- be ready for work before noon
- pay for your own hair-dressing and make-up
- the owner takes the woman's earnings; tips she may keep
- a medical check-up once a week
- no gambling

The owner pays for food and lodging. In some places more than one woman may occupy a room, but there will be a separate service room. Each woman should service several clients a night. Records of earnings are kept, and workers can withdraw money periodically. Some brothels deduct 600 baht a month from the woman's earnings as a police fee. The costs of check-ups and medical treatment must be borne by the woman. Open brothels will sell a woman's 'virginity' for as much as 20,000 baht, sometimes several times over. The brothel owner claims up to 60 per cent of this as commission.

In the beginning, part of the earned income is deducted to cover the advance paid to a woman's parents or the agent. Together with the interest and other accumulated costs, a woman must pay back double the initial outlay. Parents may also demand further advances, which will be added to the woman's debt. Some hotels employ agents who provide women for sex. Such women stay in a hotel room, and must be ready to receive clients at any time. They may offer a short-term service or an overnight session. Some women earn up to 10,000 baht a month.

Escort agencies and call-girls

Working conditions for women employed by an escort agency are superior to those in brothels. They usually serve only one client per night, whom they meet at the establishment itself or at a hotel. Clients may be Thai or foreign. Some places make an agreement with the women that they:

- will not run away
- do not gamble
- do not permit any boyfriend to come to the agency
- do not use drugs regularly or drink or smoke heavily
- have a medical check-up every week and carry a medical record card

A woman who breaks these rules will be warned. If she persists she will be fined. Playing cards or gambling with a client also makes her liable to a fine. Some agencies allow the women to reject clients, but others require that they attend any client.

Prices vary, but top-level houses will charge 10,000 baht (US$417) per night, and the women usually receive a tip as well. Some houses charge only 1,000 baht, of which 400 goes to the guide and 600 is divided equally between the owner and the woman. The average income of escorts is reported to be 10,000 baht a month. The earnings are often recorded in three books, held respectively by the owner, the woman and the client relations manager. In addition to the guide, the driver who brings the customer also receives payment. Women employed in such agencies have to pay about 500–600 baht a month for electricity, water and laundry, and 200–300 baht for medical check-ups and treatment.

A group of women from Rim Mon worked together for an agency, living in the same house. One described the working conditions thus:

> Working time is from 9 in the morning and can go through to 4 a.m. next day. We go and meet the client, perhaps at a hotel, and we stay there until he gives us permission to leave. Sometimes a client will pick up a woman at the house, or the hotel calls to say how many woman the client requires. If a client comes to the house, the madam will introduce the women. If the client is not satisfied, he may send the woman away before the time is up.

Some agencies charge lower rates for less attractive women or those who are addicts. Some are too mean to allow the woman to draw any money in advance of a date. Women who have worked for agencies often leave and become independent escorts. Longer relationships may develop with clients, and some will leave to be supported by one man. Joining an escort agency is a more desirable proposition than working in a brothel, because of the relative freedom and the higher earnings.

Massage parlours

Massage parlours are legal, and offer sex services in the guise of a massage. There is some forced prostitution here, but most women work of their own free will.

> Nuj was taken to a parlour by an agent. The first client paid 20,000 baht. She worked there for three years under close supervision. An agent picked her up from home each day and took her to work. She had between five and eight clients a day. After three years, she discovered she had saved only 5,000 baht. She was angry when she found out how little she had earned, and quarrelled with them. She was beaten by the agent.

In the massage parlour women are given a number and they sit behind a wall of glass waiting for the client to make his choice. Some parlours allow their staff to choose their clients and to reject those who refuse to wear a condom. Some customers call to reserve a particular woman, and some will take her off for several days. Massage parlours outside Bangkok provide accommodation for the women.

If she is to continue working in the massage parlour, a woman must sustain her popularity with both agents and clients. She receives about one-quarter of the fee paid by the customer. A record is kept of her earnings which she can withdraw as she requires. Some young women, particularly those from ethnic minority groups, have never withdrawn their money, but live entirely from tips.

Restaurants, tea houses and ram wong bars (traditional dance bars)

These places dissimulate the sex business by the selling of food or displays of dancing. They are registered under the Places of Entertainment Act, and this entitles them to employ women to entertain patrons. Some provide accommodation for the women, especially the tea houses and ram wong bars. The women are generally young and easy to control. Earnings depend on the location, the number of clients and tourists and the extent of the competition. The women often do not receive a wage, but get a percentage from the drinks they sell, or a fee for the shows in which they perform. A client who calls a woman to sit at his table may have to pay a fee to the bar. Our research confirmed that the workers will provide a sexual service for customers. The client pays an 'off fee', which gives him the right to take a woman out of the bar. This fee is usually 200–300 baht (US$8–12.50). Following this, they negotiate a price for sex with the woman.

Go-go bars

A number of bars in Thailand have adopted the European term 'go-go' or 'a-go-go' to advertise their business to tourists. Patpong in Bangkok and Pattaya have many such bars. Most women working in them do so voluntarily. The researchers interviewed one woman, Pum, who had been compelled by her boyfriend to dance at a bar since she was 14 to pay for his addiction to drugs.

In these bars, it is expected that women will dance partly or completely naked. They can earn extra by performing in sex shows on stage with other women or with men. Many bars have rules as to the minimum number of customers the woman must take each month. If she refuses a customer, or fails to meet her monthly target, she may be penalised by deductions from her monthly salary. She is also fined if she arrives late for work.

She is required to carry a health card and condoms. Salaries vary, according to the kind of dancing she does. Those who wear swimsuits receive 2,000 baht a month. Those who dance partly unclothed receive 2,600, and nude dancers get 3,500. By performing in sex shows, she may make between 3,000 and 4,000 baht a month, and if she does so with a male partner, both may earn 1,000 baht a night. A dancer is usually expected to buy her own costumes. Working hours are from 6 p.m. to 2 a.m.

Beer bars

Beer bars hire women to sell drinks. Customers can take a woman 'off' for a fee of 100–150 baht. Beer bars are popular in the tourist areas of Bangkok, Pattaya and Phuket. It is easy to get these jobs: neither qualifications nor references are required. The women are expected to welcome the clients and encourage them to buy drinks. Bars pay a monthly salary of between 800 and 2,000 baht, and tips may about to 10–30 baht a night. We were told that the bars expect each woman to go 'off' twice a week and not less than five times a month. Work usually starts at 6 p.m., when the bars are cleaned. Customers arrive from about 8 p.m., and bars usually close around 2 a.m., but some remain open until dawn. Some bars demand a monthly medical check-up at the employee's own expense.

> I work in a bar and live with foreigners. The neighbours didn't understand what the bar was. As far as they knew, we got commission from the drinks we sell. But if someone likes us, we'll go with him. (Pattaya)

Speaking another language is an advantage for women, who are then empowered to negotiate more favourable terms. Some customers deliberately select women who are unable to communicate with them, assuming that they are new to the business.

Sex Establishments Overseas

Working conditions and characteristics of the sex industry vary from country to country. However, some things remain constant.

Bars and cabarets

Many Thai sex workers are employed in bars overseas. This began in Germany in the 1970s, and returnees to Thailand encouraged others to go. They could stay legally in Germany for three months without a visa. Initially, Thai women working in Germany could make good money, but this has been reduced over the years. More recently, trafficking and forced prostitution have darkened the prospects.

> I went [to Germany] to sell sex. It was illegal. There was no contract and no fixed working hours. After travelling expenses and brokerage fees had been deducted, the net income from a three-month period was 100,000 baht. I worked until my visa expired, returned to Thailand, then went back again. Our lodging was on the top floor of the owner's house. The ground floor was a pub and snack bar, the first floor a cabaret, the second floor an X-rated theatre. The third floor consisted of rooms for rent, just like a brothel. The owner and his family lived on the third floor.

Thai women who worked in Germany in the early years were relatively independent. Their income was high in comparison to what they could earn in Thailand. Some had plastic surgery and changed their identity, so that they could continue to re-enter the country. Over time, working conditions changed. Some migrant women were deceived: they were told they would be selling drinks, not sex. Increasing deductions from their salaries were made for a variety of reasons – travel expenses, brokerage fees and the cost of an arranged marriage. These debts sometimes amounted to 300,000 baht, and could be increased on the whim of the bar owner.

In 1991 the German government imposed an entry visa on Thais. The cost of references and brokerage fees went up, all borne by the woman. Attempts were made to bring in Thai women as refugees, which allowed them a longer stay in the country.

We were told that in Japan women were sold off by a broker who sometimes went with them to the country. The individual who has paid the broker is called the 'money owner'. The woman must pay the money owner a debt which comes to two or three times the purchase price. The money owner, if (s)he is not the bar owner, comes to an agreement with the bar, not with the woman. Japanese bars sell food and drink, and have women welcome the customers and chat with them. A woman must be ready to leave with the customers and to have sex with them. There are around 20 women in each bar. Women working in them can be divided roughly into three groups:

- women married to Japanese men;
- women brought to Japan by bar owners and forced to service a debt;
- women purchased by a money owner.

The third group constitutes the majority, and they are subject to strict control by the money owner. They may not choose their clients and they can be sold off when repayment of their debt is almost complete. The women then begin debt payment to a new money owner. Their only income is from tips; some money owners take even the tips. The money owner may threaten her life or the life of her parents in order to intimidate her into staying with the bar. Women in the first and second groups work until their debts are paid, and they can then leave or claim for themselves the income from the sex service they provide.

Before the customers arrive, the women clean and tidy the place. Then they must welcome and entertain the customers. If there is karaoke, they must learn to sing Japanese songs. If a customer wants to take a woman off, he speaks to the madam. She has an address card which the woman can show to the taxi-driver for the return trip. The arrangement may be short-term or overnight; the price of the former is 10,000–15,000 yen (2,000–3,000 baht; about US$100) and the latter 30,000 yen. The fee is shared between the madam and the money owner.

If the client should complain about the service, the woman may be punished. If she refuses oral or anal sex, she may be scolded or beaten. If the woman is disobedient or tries to escape, she risks being beaten by thugs working for the Yakuza (Japanese mafia). The Yakuza are heavily involved in the Japanese sex industry. The woman rarely receives medical treatment or any help in avoiding illness or pregnancy. Medical costs in Japan are very high, so some women arrange to have birth-control pills sent from Thailand. During the interviews we were told that Thai bar workers with HIV/AIDS or cancer of the cervix are sent back to Thailand. If a woman's money owner incurs any medical costs, these will be added to the woman's debt.

A woman must please both her customers and the money owner. She must earn a maximum in the shortest possible time. At times of economic boom in Japan a woman can repay her debt within three months, but in a recession it may take more than a year. The debt may also be arbitrarily increased. Food and living expenses are sometimes added. Working illegally in Japan makes them more vulnerable to the inhuman treatment and abuse. Some have assaulted their money owner or madam in an attempt to escape; but they run the risk of arrest for assault as well as illegal residence. A Thai woman who killed her boss to end her slavery-like situation in Japan – the Shimodate case – said:

> Many women cried at night. Some had worked for more than five or six months, and were able to pay back only US$8,000. ... We were her slaves. Why did we let her treat us like animals? Even cattle, after hard work, have time to rest. When they fall sick, they get medical care. But we are human beings, we feel pain and misery like any other being.

Some women have become free by making a relationship with a member of the Yakuza. They may then become money owners themselves and buy other women. Some money owners have more than ten women under their control, and send them to bars in other cities. They travel between the cities to collect the money, which the bar owners keep for them.

Brothels and hotels

Of all the places which offer women for sex, working conditions in the brothels are the most oppressive. Brothel owners in Japan often impose severe restrictions on freedom of movement. The Yakuza often control, or have interests in, the brothels. Their sole motivation is profit, and they have little regard for the rights of the workers. A woman who refuses to obey the owner will be under threat of being sold to another brothel. There are stories of women who have been killed for misbehaviour.

Brothels in Germany are generally less harsh than those in Japan. However, the women often have no choice of clients, and are made to service numerous customers, at prices as low as DM30–50 (US$20–33).

Conditions in brothels in Malaysia are also severe, and they impose strict penalties for any breach of the rules. Some are reported to place the offender for a time in a blender, or cold storage room. In Singapore and Malaysia many sex businesses operate from hotels. Management charges a service fee, and shares the payment with the sex worker at a ratio of 60:40.

> [In Malaysia] I lived in a common house owned by a Chinese. In the evening I was driven to work and had many clients. I had to work hard to please them. They were worse than Thai clients. The income was poor. I earned about 190 baht, but had to pay the brokerage fee. I have no idea how much the owner took.

Sometimes a taxi-driver would bring clients to a brothel and charge them 3,000 baht. He would keep half as commission, with the remainder split between the woman and the owner. Some women, like Pring from Soi Dao, operated more independently. She took a hotel room and asked the hotel staff to refer clients to her. The fee was then shared between them.

Conditions in Hong Kong are poor. The 'owner' or manager, who may have arranged for the woman to come to Hong Kong, employs staff to escort her. She has no right to choose clients, and may expect between 13 and 30 a day. Her fee is shared with the owner, the hotel owner and the escort. She generally gets about ten per cent.

Marriage market

The mail-order bride business involves a broker who arranges a marriage between a foreigner and a Thai for a fee usually chargeable to both parties. It has been estimated that in Germany alone there are 60 such companies (Mansson 1995). The brokerage fee in Denmark may be as high as 50,000 baht. Women travel from Thailand in small groups. When they arrive, they stay in a house provided by the broker, to which local men come to choose their future wives. Until chosen, the women are locked in the house so that they do not escape. Travel expenses on top of the fee are sometimes demanded of the women. They may be sold several times over, or taken to a brothel. Marriage bureaux advertise in local Thai newspapers, enticing women to countries like Taiwan. Taiwanese criminal gangs charge up to 150,000 baht in brokerage fees. It is not uncommon for the woman to be taken directly to a brothel. (*Siam Post* 7 August 1995).

Sweatshops/factories

Factories also employ illegal migrant labour. There are closed factories in many countries, where workers are concealed from officials, and labour laws do not apply. In August 1995, a group of 68 Thai workers, mainly women, were found imprisoned in a garment factory in the USA. The conditions and wages were appalling. Many had been captive for years. They sometimes worked a 20-hour day, and the wages were 25 per cent of the legal – ungenerous – minimum. The factory owner had possession of their passports and valuables. The debt of each worker was of the order of 120,000 baht (*Thai Rath* 5 August 1995). At the time of writing, compensation claims are being pursued through the US legal system, and those responsible have been sentenced to prison terms.

Violation of human rights

Trafficking in women not only breaches the criminal and many other laws, it leaves a unique and ineradicable social legacy. The circumstances of the women's work described above represent clear violations of human rights, and have the further effect of imposing a social stigma on the women and their families.

> When she was 27, Juree travelled from Nakhon Pathom to Japan, hoping to become a nanny. She was told by a friend, who paid her travelling expenses, that a good job awaited her. When she arrived, she discovered she was the 'property' of the money owner who had financed the trip. She was taken to sex venues and coerced into sex work. She was responsible for the debt from her travel as well as daily living expenses. She was assaulted and abused by the owner of the sex establishment, and threatened with death if she should try to run away. She was later sold on to another establishment. She later learned that she was HIV-positive, and was sent back to Thailand with neither savings nor benefits.

Summary

Women are forced to work as bonded labour in payment for debts incurred during migration. They are subject to arrest for both illegal residence and illicit work. They have no automatic right to the medical or social services available to legal residents. When women are forced to sell sex, they have no power to choose their customers, or the type of sexual service they must provide. They are at high risk of HIV, and may be tested often, with neither their knowledge nor permission, and the results may be withheld from them.

Women migrants are often targets of racial discrimination. When immigration laws are enforced, and a woman is arrested for illegal residency or overstaying, no account is taken of the circumstances in which she may have travelled to the country. The use of false travel documents is a punishable offence in both the sending and receiving countries. When women seek help from officials, such as the police, they may face further violence. In court, a woman's identity is rarely concealed, which leads to more public humiliation. Children born to illegal immigrants may have no right to become citizens of their country of birth.

8

Women, Family and Community

Forced prostitution not only damages the women who work as prostitutes against their will, but also adversely affects their families and communities. The economic impact of prostitution may generate a net gain for the worker because of her earnings, or it may lead to greater indebtedness because of the percentage taken by agents, and the loss of a worker from household production. Families and communities sometimes have to defend themselves against accusations of low morality because of their complicity in the sex industry. In this chapter, we will discuss the impact of the sex trade on women, their families and communities, and the changes in relationships which their involvement in prostitution brings about.

Under Pressure

People bought us to work. I almost lost my mind when I realised I had been sold. I had a huge debt and the living conditions were bad. But when I wrote home, I had to say I was fine. (Ton Yang village)

Most women go abroad believing they have secured a well-paid job. But for those who have been deceived about the nature or conditions of their work, life can turn into a nightmare. They may find they are working for nothing, paying off inflated debts, and with little control over customers or the circumstances of their labour. Their status as illegal migrant workers adds to the pressure, since they must avoid contact with any government authorities. The women may be homesick and worried about being resold to another brothel.

[Japan] was very depressing. We couldn't do any of the things we could in Thailand. We couldn't go out, because our visas had expired. It was a very difficult time. We didn't want to do it, but we were forced to ... I do not want others to go through what we had to. Our fellow Thais treated us as though we were not human. They treated us like helpless animals. (Rim Mon village)

Tranquillisers are readily available, and are frequently used to dull the sense of shame and to ease the psychological pain of daily work.

We had to wear very revealing outfits, we had to allow customers to grab and fondle us, we had to sit in their laps. We feel guilty about problems we caused their families, because some married men become attached to us. We have no friends and we cry a lot. We are so lonesome. We drink, we take drugs to numb the pain. And the customers are free to do anything they like with us, because they have bought our time and our services.

Some women do confide in members of their family.

I have to put up with everything because of the money. I'll take home a lot, so that no one can look down on us. It's very dangerous here. Several people have died. Last week, 40 were arrested. I don't know when I'll be among those rounded up. Please have pity on me. (Khon Na village)

The majority, though, do not tell their families about the difficulties they face. They send home snaps of themselves wearing nice dresses and looking happy. They send money regularly but do not explain the source of their income. Families are often reluctant to ask. Both sides justify themselves. The community continues to express its disapproval of prostitution, even though generations of women have earned a living this way.

Women sex workers seek acceptance from the community like everyone else. Those forced into prostitution are likely to get more sympathy as 'victims', but they are not perceived as being 'nice women and virtuous wives'. They can still be dutiful daughters, however, who sell sex for money. Conspicuous wealth is seen as one way of compelling respect from fellow villagers and relatives. Some women turn the tables and buy sexual services from men.

Personal Rights and Survival of the Family

The 1960 Act for the Abatement of Prostitution makes prostitution illegal. That is to say, the selling of sex is forbidden, although the buying of sex is not. This is why prostitutes can be arrested, fined and sent to a rehabilitation centre. They are morally judged, but their customers usually escape censure. Sex workers feel they must justify their means of livelihood to society in general. They point to their duty to parents, and the material wealth they have contributed to their family's well-being. They argue that they have every right to work as prostitutes if this helps fulfil their duty of taking care of their mother and father.

> People may think we are stupid, selling our young bodies. We don't think so. It is a struggle to stay alive. We cannot bear to see our parents suffer. They brought us up. They didn't force us into it. And we have no other way of repaying them, because we have no good education and we don't come from rich or influential families who can find decent jobs for us. Our young bodies are all we have to improve the family's economic status. I don't care what other people say. Maybe Bangkok people really think what we do is wrong. But none of us thinks so. It is our life and our future. Once we have made up our mind, we have to keep on telling ourselves it is okay to do it. (Rim Mon village)

To prove their own worth, women working in the sex trade feel pressure to hurry home with their money, to display their wealth. This they do by renovating their houses or buying electrical appliances. Although they usually succeed in raising the economic status of their families, they are still aware that what they are doing is not acceptable to society.

> Many of my friends who stay behind in the village look at us in a strange way. (Rim Mon village)

> I feel inferior. I'm afraid my friends will hate me for what I'm doing. My friends talk to me all right, but we are no longer as close as before. I'm different from them. I'm no longer a virgin. I'm afraid their parents will say things about me behind my back. They may think I'm trying to lead their daughters astray. Some of my friends invite me to their houses. I don't want to go.

> I intended to enrol in a non-formal education programme together with my friends. But then I was afraid my friends would know what I've been doing. What if the teachers found out? What would I do? Fortunately, my application never got through. It was a relief.

Life is more difficult for women who could not stand the conditions of the sex trade and who returned home with limited money. At Na Thong village, two young women who returned home after a short absence found themselves unwelcome. They were forced to go away again. Local people said they had failed because they were lazy, or took to gambling, or because they had no sense of gratitude towards their family who had borrowed money to pay the agents. Prostitutes who return home because of work-related illness also face hostility. Three sick women had come back to Ton Yang village. They were shunned by the people who suspected they 'had AIDS'. A teacher at one primary school in Chiang Rai said:

While prostitutes could send money home, their parents became extravagant in their spending. But when their children got AIDS, they abandoned them, even though they had been sending enough money to feed the whole family.

Many who leave the sex trade try to start a new life. Usually they want to begin afresh in a big city where they are not known.

I used to say to a friend that I could always further my studies, but I can't. I don't think other students would want to be friends with me if they knew what I'd done.

Many women spoke of a loss of self-esteem. Others believe they have learned lessons about life the hard way.

Our experience taught us how to take care of ourselves. We have learned to judge people and read their intentions. It isn't that we have suddenly become very wise. But if we had stayed in the village, we would still be gullible rural girls.

Although these women feel they have become wiser, they do not necessarily want others to enter the sex trade.

Even though we are doing it, we don't want our sisters to follow us. The money is good, that's for sure. But it is humiliating to be used to satisfy other people's lust. Just imagine, sleeping with a man you have never seen before in your life. A man just sits there and when he points a finger at you, you have to go and sleep with him. You ask his name, and he tells you, probably not his real one. He could be a thief, or just anybody. We have chosen our way. We have to go on with it because we can't just go back to work in the fields. Once we've lost our virginity, there's no turning back. (Rim Mon village)

I tell every girl who wants to know what it's like in the sex trade. I tell them not to do what I have done. I tell my story with tears in my eyes. But they won't listen.

In the past four or five years, three women from Ton Yang village have died while working abroad.

Family Coercion

The hardship is my daughter's problem. I'm not affected by it in any way. That's all right by me. Besides, children have a duty to repay their parents. They have to struggle, make a living, earn money. They shouldn't remain idle. (Thiang of Khamwan village, near Ton Yang)

When labour first migrated to foreign countries, rural people believed such jobs could only bring good. They saw people return and build bigger houses, buy more land. This spurred a large number of male heads of households to seek work abroad. When this led to deepening debt, female family members followed the same path. It was found that in some areas in the north-east, most women workers going abroad were married. A sense of family responsibility is a decisive factor in migration.

> We want our family to be happy. I don't want my children to grow up in poverty as I did. I didn't have a happy childhood. I had to go and find odd jobs here and there to bring home some money. In any case, I also want some money for myself to avoid hardship.

From the surveys conducted in Ton Yang and Khon Na in the north-east, it emerged that whenever a family got into debt as a result of the father's migration, the mother was always the next to go. In some cases, her migration helped pay off the debt, but did not raise the family's economic status. Even more unfortunate were those women who were cheated as their husbands had been. Some had to sell their land, which forced their children to go off to look for work. In the meantime, the prostitution rings became more extensive and more sophisticated. Many parents, seeing only the positive element in the success of women working abroad, encouraged their daughters to do likewise. In spite of news reports about the dangers of migration, and warnings from some government officials, parents still go to considerable lengths to further their daughters' plans to migrate, even falsifying household records or identity cards to obtain passports.

In Na Thong, ten mothers of young women who went to Japan said they had been led to believe that their daughters would earn the equivalent of 20,000 baht (US$830) a month as waitresses. Some borrowed 25,000 baht and gave it to an agent. They heard nothing from their daughters for a long time, but were reluctant to seek help from the authorities, because they had been warned beforehand, and feared they might be charged with a criminal offence. They tried to contact their daughters through the agent. Initially, all the mothers wanted their daughters back as soon as possible, but most changed their minds when the money began to arrive.

> Now I want my daughter to live there legally, with a valid visa and passport. I don't want her back yet. She can find work anywhere, as long as she gets the money she wants.

One mother who had wanted her daughter back immediately said:

I don't want my daughter to be a prostitute. If I had known, I wouldn't have
sent her there.

The expectation of parents that their daughter must contribute to
enhancing the economic status of the family, even if that means working
in prostitution, reflects a major change in attitude. When parents insist
that children must pay them back with money for their upbringing, this
suggests that the relationship has become commercialised. Many young
women feel that their primary purpose is to provide material comfort
to the rest of the family:

> I have many problems. Everybody in the family wants to borrow money
> when they know I have some cash. Some of them simply beg. Father, mother,
> brother-in-law, sisters – they all want money. That's why I never let them
> know if I have any. They never pay it back. For them it's easy money. They're
> extravagant and it is all used up in no time. They dump all their problems
> on me. My sister is having her baby in an expensive private hospital, my
> sister-in-law just had a miscarriage, my nephew is sick, father and mother
> want allowances, my brother wants a new car and another sister is building
> a house. (Rim Mon)

> They think it's easy for me to make a lot of money so they can help me spend
> it. They don't have to struggle to make a living. They just wait for me to
> throw my money around.

Changes in the Family

If a woman goes away as a sex worker, whether voluntarily or under
duress, and regularly sends money home, she is considered successful.
If she fails to send home substantial sums, the family says she is a victim
of the sex trade. One mother in Na Thong said, 'The trade in humans
is one where he or she has to work for nothing.' Families are nearly
always defensive about the work of their daughters.

* Families may refuse to disclose the nature of the job. Although
  members of the family know that a daughter is working as a
  prostitute, they will tell neighbours that she is working as a waitress,
  housemaid or bar-tender. They will show snapshots of their
  daughter, modestly dressed, in a well-furnished flat with friends, or
  posing in front of a luxury car.
* They may react aggressively. When neighbours start to gossip about
  the truth behind a daughter's migration, families may spring
  aggressively to their defence. Da, the daughter of a former village
  head of Khon Na, was the first woman from the village to work as

a prostitute in Japan, but her family will not admit that this is the work she does.

- They may start to spend conspicuously. Conspicuous consumption includes throwing big parties for family members, buying electrical equipment, such as a refrigerator or washing machine, and building a modern house. This material wealth compels a certain respect from the community. Social position is further enhanced if the family is able to lend money to others.

- Families of prostitutes may seek acceptance by donating money or materials to the local temple or school. By accepting such donations, these institutions lend some legitimacy to the way the money is earned. The parents of Puen and Phaeng donated a refrigerator and a substantial sum to the local temple. Another family in Soi Dao organised a fair to raise funds for the local temple.

Family relationships have changed significantly in terms of hierarchy and gender roles. Traditionally, the father and other senior male members of the family held most power over decision-making. This has been changed to some degree by the increasingly obvious contribution of women to the rise in family status through labour migration. In some families, women are now effectively household heads, and they have a greater share in making decisions. Parents have even come to respect their daughters.

> In the past, we didn't even have a house of our own. We lived with relatives who didn't really want us because we were so poor. Now it's different. Nobody discriminates against us any more. Everyone is pleased to see us.

Parents may wield less power over their daughters' decisions and choices. This contrasts with the − not distant − past, when parents were the decision-makers in all things.

> In the past, nobody dared to go out of the village to work. Helping your parents in the field was enough. Even if some of us badly wanted to go and work elsewhere, we wouldn't go if our parents didn't allow it. (Rim Mon)

Now a family with several daughters is considered lucky. A community leader of Rim Mon said, 'Some parents remain idle, just waiting for money from their daughters'.

Relationships between husbands and wives have also changed. The husband of a woman who goes abroad for sex work has to give up his dominant role in the household. This is common in the north-east, where most of those who migrate for prostitution are married women. There are a number of cases in Na Thong and Ton Yang where wives are getting divorced so that they can marry foreign boyfriends. One husband in Ton Yang was offered 150,000 baht (US$6,250) if he would consent to a divorce. Another man still lives with his ex-wife after their divorce, on condition that he removes himself when her Japanese husband visits. The acceptability of otherwise 'immoral' conduct is attributable to the superior claims of economics. As the ex-husband of a woman who married a German after working in Germany said, 'The villagers think of nothing but money'. Husbands of most prostitutes abroad start sexual relationships with other women in the absence of their wives. Some plunder the money the women send home and spend it on gambling. Such behaviour contributes to the high divorce-rate.

Migration of women has a great impact on children. Many families are kept together by the children. Thom, whose wife went to Japan for more than seven years, said 'I live for my child'. One child of a woman migrant worker wanted her mother back, and would prefer to see her father go abroad.

Father is a man and can take care of himself. Mother is a woman who is weaker. She could get sick. We are worried about her.

Many women come back to find their relationship with their children has changed. They often feel they have grown apart.

I never gave them motherly love and human warmth. I only sent money. I don't know what to do. I'm thinking I'll tell them if I hadn't gone away to work, they would never have had the chance of a proper education.

To provide a good future for their children is the main reason given by women who go to work abroad. The fact that their mother is a prostitute may have a strong influence on the choice of career of their children, especially daughters. Some schoolteachers in the north report that prostitutes tend to attach less importance to education, valuing material wealth and conspicuous consumption more highly. There are examples of families where three generations of women have been in prostitution.

The Changing Community

The community judges people by their wealth. Sri has a Japanese husband who visits her in Ton Yang.

When we were poor, we used to beg help from relatives and friends. They would turn a deaf ear, even though they were in a position to help us. But when we have money, they are always coming to visit us. They suddenly want to be friends. They have to accept us, even though they may not have a very high opinion of us. But they have to come to see us. (Ton Yang)

Social interaction is to some degree determined by material success.

It seems that the traditional way of life, characterised by mutuality and interdependence, is being replaced by a competitive materialism. Poorer members of the community must struggle hard in order to gain acceptance from others.

> Before we went to Japan we were looked down on by people in the village simply because we were poor. Now they treat us nicely, and have a high opinion of us. I never thought money could have such power over people. (Ton Yang)

> My mother never had a sarong. She wore only a ragged cloth. No one ever invited her to any village fair or feast. I once heard someone say she didn't want to invite my mother because she was so dirty. I was very angry. I thought to myself, if and when I have enough money, I will buy her nice clothes to wear. Now that is what I'm doing. They have started inviting her to all kinds of social functions, weddings, house-warming parties. Before, we never really had any social life. Now people go out of their way to talk to us and treat us well. Suddenly, we are very much one of them. (Rim Mon)

This leads some women to conclude that the only way to win acceptance from the community is to raise their family's economic status. In communities such as Rim Mon, where migration for prostitution is long established, the women believe that the community no longer considers prostitution to be immoral.

> Before, when only a few women went into prostitution, people may have looked down on prostitutes. But now many women join the sex trade. And they come back to the village with their car and jewellery. People no longer criticise them.

This apparent optimism about acceptance from the community may be at odds with reality.

> They show disapproval if the women come back and behave differently, wear tight clothes and so on. And most men wouldn't consider marrying a former prostitute, because they feel they cannot trust them. They suspect they will go back to prostitution when they become bored with domestic life. (Soi Dao)

> By all accounts, these women must have four or five husbands at a time. And they have no patience. They can't live with one man for long because they know they can earn a lot of money and don't have to depend on anyone. Even if some man would marry them, he wouldn't be able to stand the idea of his wife sleeping with other men for money.

They don't want to work hard with a shovel or spade and earn less than 100 baht a day. We must change their attitude towards work.

Some are more sympathetic.

They only want to get rich. Nothing wrong with that. If I were in their position, I'd probably do the same thing. Maybe it can't be helped.

The community rarely criticises those who encourage or compel women to go into prostitution. On the contrary, these people are treated with respect. In Rim Mon and Ton Yang, the agents are popular among local people.

The Role of Community Leaders

In Rim Mon, where there has been mass migration of women to work as prostitutes, Buddhist monks, teachers and local administrators tend to have different responses to the issue. Teachers are more likely to see prostitution as a social problem, rather than as a problem of the individual or family.

Prostitution is an immoral way of life, and should not be accepted by the community. Those who encourage or force people into it must be punished. We are not saying that women who become prostitutes are bad people. Many do it because they have no choice. But I condemn those who encourage or allow these girls to become prostitutes. These are horrible people.

Many teachers are disheartened because they have failed to protect their pupils from the organisers and recruiters of prostitutes.

It makes you feel bad about being a teacher. You try to convince your pupils, especially the girls, that to become a prostitute is shameful, and that they should not even consider it as a choice. Several of my pupils have become prostitutes anyway. I told the rest of them that if they do likewise, I wouldn't speak to them again. A number of others went ahead just the same. And when they came back, they told me how they had succeeded in raising their family's social and economic status through their self-sacrifice. What am I supposed to do? (Rim Mon)

A campaign against child prostitution run by the Foundation for Women in Rim Mon since 1987, and renewed government interest in suppressing child prostitution, have revived the optimism of the teachers. They consistently tell parents and pupils that 'cultivation of the mind is a better way to solve problems than seeking material wealth'.

Buddhist monks should in principle be opposed to prostitution; but

there has been little evidence of their involvement in activities to change
the attitudes of the people.

> We must draw up our plan carefully, because we need co-operation from
> many groups of people before we can tackle the problem effectively. (Abbot
> of Rim Mon)

Rather than actively engaging with the issue, temples are accepting
donations from brothels.

> We must be reasonable. We must ask ourselves whether the operators of
> places of entertainment who come to make merit at the temple are recruiting
> the girls to work with them. What we see is girls applying in droves to do
> the work. Besides, what is wrong if the employers of the girls make merit at
> the local temple or visit the village? (Abbot of Rim Mon)

This attitude is symptomatic of those who offer protection to agents who
recruit girls for prostitution. By accepting donations from brothel
operators, the temple confers legitimacy on their business. The former
headmaster of the local school, however, refused donations from
prostitutes, because he feared that the school would appear to condone
prostitution.

The village head of Rim Mon is a former recruiting agent for brothels.
He believes that the government's agricultural projects and job-creation
programmes do not attract the women, because they can make much
more money out of prostitution. The village head helped to raise the
status of former prostitutes by appointing them members of a committee
for women's affairs. In selecting applicants, he stated that committee
members must be 'pretty, rich and own a car'.

In other communities we surveyed, social organisations showed little
interest in the problem of migration for prostitution. Instead, community
leaders, such as village heads, tend to play an active role in encouraging
women to go into such work. In Ton Yang, the daughter of the village
head recruited young women for work in Japan, and later followed them.
Most village heads have minor wives, or *mia noi*. (According to Thai
Family Law, polygamous relationships are forbidden. A husband must,
de jure, have only one wife, but in practice he may have a number of wives,
without any legal sanction.) In Na Thong, the village head resisted a
campaign to publicise the sex trade among villagers. He feared he might
be punished for allowing young women to be lured into prostitution.

During the second phase of the research project, however, some
changes in attitude were observed. These can be attributed to
government policy on child prostitution, and to the work of the
researchers themselves, together with local women. The village head and

teachers in Rim Mon supported the project to create alternative employment for former prostitutes. Previously, this project had been carried out away from the community to protect those who took part from any stigma. In Ton Yang and Na Thong, parents of prostitutes, former sex workers, and girls who have just finished school, are working collectively to promote an understanding of migration and what it means (see Chapter 9).

Summary

In Thailand, deceit, threats of violence, and actual violence against women are all part of the trade in women for sex. Migration for prostitution has been transformed into sex trafficking in the form of forced prostitution and arranged liaisons. Trade within the country usually involves a cash payment to the family by brothel owners, whereas the international trade usually involves payment by the family or the woman to agents. Women who want to work as prostitutes abroad are reduced to commodities to be sold in the transnational sex market. Apart from oppressive working conditions, their status as illegal residents makes their livelihood a precarious one. They face abuse for the work they do as well as the everyday racism of which all migrant workers are victims. They are subject to family pressure to provide more and more money, and are denied the consolation of doing work which their parents can be proud of. Many women find escape from these contradictions in drugs.

When the money starts to arrive, perceptions of prostitution are modified sufficiently to encourage more and more women to consider migration for sex work, with the open consent of their families. Certain illusions are maintained about the conditions of work, and these, in turn, compel the women to remain silent on the deceit and abuse which they must endure.

To combat the trade in women for prostitution, government agencies must play a major role in raising awareness. This includes the spread of information about the facts, the provision of counselling for women who are thinking of migration, and work with families and communities in order to build alternatives to leaving home. Assistance and support must be available for women who have been mistreated, and greater efforts made to detain and punish those responsible for deceit and abuse.

9

From Research to Action

The second phase of the Research and Action project on Traffic in Women (RATW), from November 1993 to October 1994, focused on working co-operatively with women in their communities to address the issue of trafficking. The primary objective was to identify appropriate strategies, both at the village level and nationally, to combat the traffic in women. The approach was to be participatory, that is, led by the people most directly affected by trafficking. The role of the research team was to assist with devising and developing such strategies. This was to include spreading information, raising awareness, and organising groups to decide on and to implement the strategies. This chapter details the results of this phase of the project.

Three villages were selected; the choice was based on the extent of trafficking and on the degree of interest shown by village women. Project activities were also pursued in the urban centres of Bangkok and Pattaya. In the north, the project team worked in Rim Mon village, which had a long history of migration for prostitution and a large number of returned sex workers. In the north-east, Ton Yang village was included, but Khon Na was replaced by a neighbouring village, 'Na Thong'. Na Thong was the home of 15 young women trafficked to Japan between 1989 and 1991, and the mothers of these women had contacted the research team for assistance in bringing them home. This seemed a good starting point from which to develop strategies for resistance to trafficking. In Pattaya, the researchers worked with local sex workers; in Bangkok, mostly with agency personnel.

Mothers in Na Thong Village

When the research team first visited Na Thong, ten mothers there had lost contact with daughters who had gone to Japan. They wanted help in bringing their daughters home. They had borrowed money, sold cattle or mortgaged land to pay the broker's fee of 25,000 baht (US$1,042). The broker, who lived locally and was a relative of one mother, had told them that their daughters would be working in a restaurant for 20,000 baht a month. The women now believed that they were working as prostitutes. The promised remittances had failed to arrive, and the debts incurred at home were still unpaid. The mothers did not dare ask for assistance from government officers, because they had been warned against sending their daughters away.

A public tribunal on traffic in women, organised by the Asian Women's Human Rights Council, was held in Tokyo in March 1994, and this provided an opportunity for the group to talk openly about their experiences. The research team had suggested that they send a representative to Tokyo, and Nee was elected as spokesperson.

Before she went, Nee met all the mothers to discuss their experiences. Some had already changed their minds about wanting their daughters to return, either because they had heard from them in the meantime or because they had received money from Japan. One daughter had written to her mother, warning her to trust nobody. This frightened others, who decided to leave things alone. During her visit to Japan, Nee met migrant workers, visited agencies which help migrants, and visited Thai women imprisoned for killing their money-lender. She came to understand more about the difficulties faced by illegal migrant workers, and about Thai women coerced into working as prostitutes in bars and clubs.

With assistance from a local agency, Mizura, and the Japanese police, Nee found her daughter. She had just finished paying off her debt and had become a sex worker in a restaurant. The local media covered the work of the tribunal and Nee's search for her daughter. When Nee returned with her daughter to Na Thong, she told others about the working conditions and the contracts which bound the workers. A public discussion was held in Na Thong, led by Nee, and attended by people from neighbouring villages. She inspired others to write to their daughters, asking for the truth about their work in Japan. Some were shocked to learn that their daughters were employed as sex workers, but others were more pragmatic about the need to earn fast money.

The 300 people who attended the first meeting saw a video and slides dealing with the circumstances in which migrant Thai women live in Japan. For a majority, this was the first they had heard or seen of the reality. Similar meetings were held in the district and provincial centres, where Nee was joined by a number of returned women migrants, who spoke of their experiences in Singapore and Japan. These meetings were well attended, and there were requests for Nee to visit other districts where the emigration rate was high. A returned migrant from Rim Mon in the north came to one meeting, and went back to her village to organise a women's group there.

Community Reaction

Reactions to the meetings and the disclosure of the conditions in which women were living were not all positive or compassionate. One woman complained:

> Nee said too much. She should not say that our daughters are prostitutes and suffer misfortune. Some believe their daughters are doing the right thing. Nee talked too much because she wanted others to believe her. Staying a few days there, how could she know the country thoroughly?

Others, who had received money from their daughters, were angry because they now knew how it had been earned. One suggested Nee should go and work in Japan herself. This anger reflected the strength of the social and moral divisions between 'good girls' and 'bad girls'. The same attitude compels returned women to remain silent about their experiences. Many returnees do not stay in their home villages, but prefer to go and live elsewhere in Thailand.

Communities do not necessarily support those who have been forced into prostitution. Following Nee's personal disclosure about her daughter's experience, some villagers blamed the daughter. The researchers also became targets for anger. One government officer accused the research team of humiliating the young women for their own ends. The village head, who was related to Nee, told her to desist because it brought disgrace on the family, and hence upon him also. These reactions made the research team more cautious about using local women to recall their experiences in public. The presentation of such stories clearly runs the risk of exposing them to possible further abuse.

It is clear that much of the traffic in women remains in shadow, and that a collusive unknowing sometimes unites families with agents, traffickers and exploiters. While the whole nexus remains hidden, face may be saved; but the young women must suffer in secrecy and silence.

The Migrant Women's Network

Following the provincial meeting in Nong Khai, three women who had been abused by traffickers and employers worked with the research team to record their personal histories. All these women, Mali, Chantra and Duangta, also organised groups in their home villages to spread awareness of migration and trafficking. The telling of their stories gave them real comfort, because, in doing so, they came to perceive that what had happened to them was only part of wider social and economic processes, and was not a consequence of personal error or fault. They were able to understand the relationship between individual experience and the unbalanced social and economic conditions of men and women, rich and poor, both nationally and internationally.

Ton Yang village information centre

Experience gained from activities in Na Thong village clarified the need to make known what life is really like for migrant women. Mali, who had worked in Singapore, started a group with the purpose of educating the people of Ton Yang, and a neighbouring village, 'Kham Wan'. This group was supported by the research project, especially with books and videos about migration, prostitution and the kind of life women can expect when they work in foreign countries. Members of the group started discussions after women had given testimony about their own experiences, the sufferings and sorrows they had endured.

The reaction from young people taking part was very powerful. Many said they would never go overseas in search of work now that they had some idea of what to expect. The women themselves, when they came to reflect on these sessions, struck up a strong rapport with their audiences.

> The way Thai prostitutes in Japan are treated is depressing. People are not aware it is like this. You feel sad for the parents whose daughters have gone away to work. It would be all right if they knew the sacrifices their daughters are making, if they knew the real cost of the money they earn. It is very sad for the parents who do not know.
>
> The ones who went abroad came back and built a big house; they have more money to spend. Some people still want to follow them. Migration brings problems to the community.

The women and young people in Ton Yang agreed to set up an information centre. To begin with, this was done in Mali's living room but later, they extended her house to provide a space for reading matter and information relating to migration. Government officers have also contributed documentary material. Among visitors to the centre have been people from Na Thong, who are keen for something similar in their village.

More and more women and men approached Mali, seeking advice

on migration or information about what they could do when employment contracts were not fulfilled. Mr Kham and his friend sought her help following their deportation from New Zealand, when they had paid large fees to brokers on the promise of agricultural jobs. Mali suggested they sue the broker's company. In spite of this experience, they were still anxious to migrate far for work, because, they said, the wages in neighbouring countries were too low. Brokers are quick to promote new destinations with promises of even greater potential earnings.

The existence of the centre and the work of the group have made Mrs Tan, who is the mother of Paeng and Peaun, unhappy. It has interfered with her work of recruitment for her daughters in Japan (see Chapter 5). Her youngest daughter has even joined the group.

Returned migrants group in Rim Mon

While Ton Yang and Na Thong saw women leave for what turned out to be sex work abroad, the people of Rim Mon observed foreigners coming to their village for sex. Women with experience of sex work overseas were coming back to Rim Mon having amassed considerable wealth. Some were being supported by foreign men. It was assumed that those who had not yet returned had been less successful.

The researchers worked with some of these women in Rim Mon, particularly with those who had experienced discrimination when they came home, or who were still suffering from the trauma of working abroad.

Kham Por had been forced into prostitution by the Yakuza in Japan. She had tried to escape, but only when a Japanese customer paid her debt was she allowed to leave. She lived as the second wife of this man, but when her baby died, she came home. Her husband still visits her and gives financial support. Kham Por suffers from nightmares that the Yakuza are still after her. She has been in hospital several times. The villagers think she is neurotic. After revisiting Kham Por in 1996, the Foundation for Women learned that she had been forced to disown her baby, and to pass it over to the Japanese wife, so that the child should not end up as illegitimate under Japanese law.

Kham Por sought out the researchers, because she was sorely in need of friends. Later, she was elected president of the returned women's group. The village head could see the potential power of the group, if only because they were better off than most, but he would not offer his support. He was cynical about migrant women workers.

> If they need money, they just go south, or send their daughters. It's more comfortable than bag-weaving until their backs ache.

Kham Por started to teach other returned women, and was involved in planning vocational training for young women villagers. This had to stop when she went back into hospital.

Kham Por had introduced the researchers to other returned women, who provided valuable information which would either validate or deny the evidence collected in the first phase of the project. Most of these women had been outside the mainstream of village life. In spite of the obvious benefit the village had received from remittances, the women who had been the instruments of making this money were sometimes rejected. They were asked to help out at Songkran (the traditional Thai new year festival), because they could afford the elaborate Thai costumes required for the ceremony. In talking with the researchers, these women were able to speak of their dissatisfactions with their life as returnees, and to identify a possible new role for themselves.

> We should work with the housewives' group, because there are no other appropriate groups or programmes for women in the village.

> I would like it if there were other work for the people in our community.

> I wish that women in the community could cook properly so that we could welcome visitors, and not feel inferior. And it's a pity they don't know better manners when it comes to eating.

The researcher contacted government agencies to arrange for instruction in cookery. Field visits to other women's groups were organised. In the event, the members of the group decided that the high cost of investment in food production and the limited market were against them. They moved on to look at other ideas.

> Women need to learn and understand other people's skills and tricks of the trade, because women have to work also.

> If women are not developed, how can the country be developed?

> We are the women of a new age, we can do what we want by ourselves. We don't have to wait for men. We can do it, but we have never been given the opportunity.

They learned that working together is effective, and earns respect. Even the village head changed his mind and lent his support to the group.

> When we worked together and showed how useful we are to the village, people appreciated us more. Women came to understand that responsibility has to be shared. Although each one had to help herself, she also needed to

contribute to the wider group. In the meetings, everyone had the right to express her opinion. There was no need to whisper behind our hands.

Visits to other women's groups encouraged and strengthened their resolve. They named themselves the Women's Development Group, Rim Mon village. Following Duangta's visit to the north-east, they organised a seminar on migration and prostitution in co-operation with the local sub-district committee and the Community Development Division of the Ministry of the Interior. The seminar was titled 'Unemployment after the farming season'. Those who took part agreed that the main reason for migration was poverty, and lack of knowledge on how to make and market other produce. The success of the meeting led them on to other activities, and women from neighbouring villages began to talk about the way the traffic in women affected their own communities.

Benefits of Participation

The idea behind participatory research, and especially feminist research, is that through collective working, women will be able to articulate problems and work together on solutions. It was most clearly successful in Rim Mon, partly because the women there had not previously formed themselves into a collective entity. In Ton Yang and Na Thong, vocational groups had been established earlier. In Rim Mon, the practice of pooling and sharing ideas was new for some women. Most had had direct experience of prostitution, and this gave life and authenticity to the discussions. The researchers did not have to provide information on trafficking, as was the case with some other groups; and this left the women free to focus more on the process of working together in groups.

The group in Ton Yang consisted mainly of women who were anxious about the issue in relation to the fate of their children. The history of sex work migration in Ton Yang can be traced back to a single individual – a woman called Pang – returning from Japan, who set about recruiting others. The story runs that she brought home a million baht; and this is said to have convinced parents that big money was there for the making in Japan. More recently, two other women came back, also with considerable wealth. The members of the group felt that they had to make sure that people in the village received a more balanced picture than this rosy view of easy money. They arranged video and slide presentations on trafficking and migration, and these were followed by discussions.

These children face many difficulties, they have to endure a great deal.

The girls had to put up with whatever they found there but the parents at home thought they were having a good time. They believed what their children wrote and told them.

Stories from real life inspired those taking part to devise concrete solutions that could actually be put into practice in the village. In Na Thong, there had been many women's development activities, but none which concentrated on finding solutions through collective effort. The group started soon after the meetings which Nee had organised. One of the more popular seminars was about the law and legal procedures in foreign countries, and the kinds of help which migrant workers can draw on. This was also the first time that men had taken part in large numbers.

Spreading information

The second phase of the research confirmed that many villages lacked accurate information on migration – how it came about, what would happen to those who left, the pitfalls as well as the advantages. This was, therefore, a major focus of the women's energies. Activities included:

- core group members who had been directly caught up in trafficking, and who spoke about their personal experiences;
- researchers and others who could give out accurate information on legal issues – labour regulations, immigration laws, marriage to foreigners and the support available to children;
- documentary videos on child labour, prostitution, migration and trafficking;
- printed material – books, posters, picture books;
- presentation of the real life stories of trafficked women.

Other events included debates between children on the issues, and role-play on the stories in the books. Everything was designed to promote two-way communication, and to build understanding of all the implications of migrant sex work.

Changes in attitude and behaviour

The overwhelming impression people have of work in Japan is that it pays well. Women were sending home enough money to buy land and to renovate houses. Parents were unaware of the dangerous and damaging circumstances in which their daughters were working.

> I never thought it was cruel. I only knew that she sent a lot of money home. (Ton Yang)

> Seeing the video gave her sleepless nights. She was unhappy to see Thai girls being hit and even killed. She was afraid she would see her own daughter on the video. (Na Thong)

The reality of the conditions of work was shrouded in silence. Even returnees rarely spoke of their experiences, preferring to collude with the illusion that everything was fine. Families continued to borrow money and to mortgage their land to pay agents' fees. As they came to learn more about the life of migrant women workers, and the routine sexual exploitation they suffered, the enthusiasm of people became tempered; they showed more compassion.

> I feel sorry for those who went away to work, and who risked their lives, lost their virginity for money. If only I had known this before, I would not have let them go. (Na Thong)

During the courses of the research, people came to talk about doing things differently. Young people said they would be more cautious in seeking work outside the village. Wealthier families spoke of furthering their children's education before they would permit them to look for work. In Na Thong, the youth leader reported that all the students who finished their six years of compulsory education that year went on to secondary school. The circumstances that led young people to want to leave still existed, but it was hoped that the new awareness that had come might make them more alert and think twice before leaving home. By the time the project was concluded in Na Thong, women were still leaving for work abroad, but it was found that they were now applying to travel legally, through the Department of Labour. The destination now was more likely to be Taiwan than Japan. The women most immediately involved with the project gained confidence from working with others, and were more ready to contact agencies for assistance. They became more hopeful that they would be instrumental in effecting change.

Vocational activities

Apart from alerting people to the reality of migration for sex work, the women's groups saw the urgent need for wider local work opportunities for women and girls. In Na Thong, they gave this priority over everything else, and focused on the weaving group. In Ton Yang and Rim Mon, they combined vocational skills and the spread of information. They did not expect vocational projects to lead to a wider range of new work possibilities.

Weaving group in Na Thong: Early in the Na Thong discussions, one woman community leader mentioned the availability of interest-free loans for income-generating projects from the Community Development Department of the Interior Ministry. The women thought that reviving traditional weaving skills, using the local designs of their area, might be a possible means of creating extra income. The researchers helped with the application for the loan, and arranged visits to existing weaving groups. When no response came from the Community Development Department, the researcher suggested taking a low-interest loan from elsewhere. But the group, fearful of further debt, became discouraged. They decided to disband the weaving group, at least until the harvest was over.

Sewing group in Ton Yang: The women's group was attracted by sewing, and contacted the Non-Formal Education Department for training. They could use equipment they already owned, but needed a wider market for selling the garments. They pursued this for a time, but when demand dropped away, the sewing project was abandoned.

The experience of these two groups demonstrates the obstacles to local employment-creation, including delays in obtaining loans, the lack of outlets for products, and the absence of organising skills for co-operative enterprises.

Bag-making in Rim Mon: Vocational training in Rim Mon served as a means of bringing women together to talk about migration. Income-generating work was used to get the group to work in harmony, although the income was not the main purpose of the group. The women worked well together, and there was talk of extending the idea to other groups within the village. The alternative emphasis in this group, whereby the dynamics of the group took precedence over income-generation, is, in part, the key to its success. The Rim Mon women were, in general, better off than the other groups, so they could afford to adopt a more relaxed attitude towards additional earnings. For the others, improvement in finances was a major consideration, and the obstacles to this led to frustration and conflict.

Casework assistance

Help and counselling with individual problems was part of the overall purpose of the project. The benefits extend beyond the particular family: the example helps to win credibility and support from other people in the village and community leaders.

Assistance with documents: The difficulties over arranging documents for migrants were similar in all villages. These included government officers who demanded unofficial additional payments for preparing documents. People were often confused about which documents were required, and in what language they should be drawn up. The researchers were able to help with translations, and they accompanied villagers on their visits to government offices. The presence of researchers inhibited the officials from demanding extra fees. The confusion over official documents and correct government procedures leads to a situation which traffickers can easily exploit.

Locating women abroad: The researchers, in collaboration with staff from the Foundation for Women, helped parents trace daughters who had disappeared overseas. Some searches were happily concluded, others ended with the sad news that the women had died. There were many cases where parents had lost contact with their daughters.

Applications for scholarships: One means of combating the traffic in women is by prolonging the education of girls. The advantages are twofold: they are kept busy with study, and at the same time they are enhancing their skills for when they enter the labour market. For poor families, keeping children at school beyond the compulsory limit is too costly. In the second phase of the research, 12 scholarships were provided from project funds, and these were offered to young girls thought to be vulnerable to recruiters.

Tuition: The researchers helped young women with literacy. They also ran typing classes in Na Thong, particularly Thai/English typing skills. The equipment for this was provided by the Foundation for Women. The enthusiasm for acquiring new skills and becoming literate, especially among young women, gives some indication of the reservoir of unmet need for further education and the desire to work outside traditional agricultural labour. Some women returning from abroad hesitated before joining classes run by the Non-Formal Education Division.

> I want to study, but I don't want to be in a large class. I am shy. If the government officer is the teacher, I won't study. (Rim Mon)

The officers were impatient with this.

> We don't understand why they are shy. They've worked in Bangkok and other places. They shouldn't be shy.

The researchers tried an approach that would put them at ease. Their teaching was based upon an exchange of ideas and feelings. Many young women acknowledged this.

> At first I was shy, but now if there is anything to learn, I will do it. Reading develops our minds.

Obstacles Encountered

The project encountered some hostility, particularly from those families receiving money from daughters overseas.

> Why are you concerned with other people's business? If they want to go, what does it matter? It's better to go and earn money to spend than to stay home and starve. (Ton Yang)

The promotion of understanding had to be structured in such a way that it did not offend families whose daughters were abroad, and so that it did not add to the discrimination against returned sex workers.

One unanticipated outcome of the project was that recruitment agents and brokers were praised and congratulated by families who felt their daughters had been successful. This was the opposite of the response of those women whose stories featured in the videos and books. In Rim Mon in particular, from where there is a well-beaten path to overseas prostitution, there were many wealthy returned women. Their very presence was an eloquent denial of the message which the project was seeking to convey.

> This job is not a mistake. Right now, money can save our lives, never mind our honour. Disparaging prostitution only makes villagers dissatisfied, especially the parents of the women in prostitution.

The researchers had to make clear the difference between trafficking and prostitution. Traffic, it was explained, was about coercing women into prostitution, or into any other work, denying them adequate wages and dignified working conditions.

Participation of External Agencies

Local government personnel

Officials co-operated with and, in some cases, took part in the activities surrounding the project. Local community development officers assisted by advertising the seminars. Senior officers chaired some meetings. They were clearly familiar with the problems of migration and trafficking, but, so far, no official programmes have been set up to deal with the issue. The work of the women's groups gave them a chance to become involved without waiting for official permission.

In Rim Mon, the local teachers had already been working against trafficking and child prostitution. They had set up a counselling project specifically for girls at risk, and had arranged exhibitions illustrating the dangers of child prostitution. They had also gone with students to Bangkok for college entrance exams, and helped with applications for scholarships designed to prevent poorer children from dropping out of school. They were supported in this by the District Education Office. They reported that a higher proportion of girls are now completing their six years of compulsory education and going on to further study.

The Community Development Department has also given practical help by offering interest-free loans for income-generating schemes. This worked well in Rim Mon, as reported above, but delays in approval in Udon Thani province prevented any benefit being derived from it in Na Thong. The need for loans in Rim Mon confirms the observation that remittances from women's work in urban centres or overseas were being used mainly for capital expenditure – repairing houses or buying white goods – and little of the money was saved. A few women had started a convenience store with their earnings, but, overall, the money was deployed on conspicuous consumption and the flaunting of wealth.

Central government activity

The beginning of the FFW project coincided in 1992 with a government crackdown on child prostitution. The Chuan Leekpai Government gave the primary responsibility for the fight against child prostitution to the Department of Public Welfare. The Department set up a committee to oversee the achievement of this objective. This committee distributed a manual to the agencies involved, with an outline of their campaign and ideas for co-operative efforts. The National Commission on Women's Affairs, part of the Office of the Prime Minister, also formed a committee to inquire into the sex entertainment business.

Social programmes: The Government established social programmes to focus on women who have worked in the sex industry. These include the 'welfare home' of the Department of Public Welfare, for women released into their custody following conviction on criminal charges related to prostitution. Other aspects of the programme include vocational training, both for convicted women and for young people considered to be at risk.

Educational programmes: The Education Department provided opportunities for further education for young people, through scholarship programmes and 'welfare schools' for girls at risk. The scholarships were established in the northern provinces, from where many girls migrate for sex work, and where there are limited places in secondary schools.

Media Projects: The Department of Public Welfare published information for families on child prostitution and trafficking. The Ministry of Foreign Affairs also ran a media campaign on illegal migration to Japan, intended to inform and deter potential migrants.

Legal Programmes: The national strategy in terms of the law was to foster greater co-operation and co-ordination between government departments in implementing existing laws. These departments included Public Welfare, Provincial Administration, Foreign Affairs and the Police.

Perhaps more significant was the drafting of a bill to reform the 1960 Abatement of Prostitution Act. Non-governmental organisations lobbied vigorously in favour of the decriminalisation of prostitution, and harsher penalties against traffickers and the clients of child prostitutes. The bill did include more rigorous punishment for procurers and for the clients of under-age prostitutes, and a reduction in penalties for adult prostitutes. This bill was enacted in December 1996, and is now in force.

A second bill currently before Parliament seeks to replace the 1928 Anti-Trafficking Act, which would extend protection to boys, and provide for assistance rather than punishment for victims of trafficking. Penalties for trafficking would also be increased. This bill still awaits the final reading and approval by Parliament. (January 1997)

Health programmes: The Ministry of Public Health screens prostitutes for sexually transmitted diseases, including HIV. There have been difficulties in offering this service to immigrant sex workers, mainly because of the lack of translation and interpretation facilities. The Ministry has also surveyed the sex industry, with a view to targeting its programmes more effectively.

Following an evaluation of these projects, a number of limitations were identified. Vocational and educational support programmes have been set up only in the northern provinces. This takes no account of the existence of child prostitution and trafficking in other regions, notably in the north-east. The vocational programme of the Public Welfare

Department provided skills-training to 2,000 young women a year. The average income generated by this amounted to between 60 and 150 baht per day (US$2.50–6.25), which was considered too low to sustain a commitment by the young women to the work. Participants complained that the skills they acquired were limited and not adapted to their needs. Many were not convinced that prostitution was a bad choice of occupation. The Department of Industry also ran a skills-training programme in an effort to resist child prostitution. It set up projects in 72 villages, but only 1,363 individuals completed the programme, and, of these, only 262 were girls between the ages of 13 and 18.

Non-governmental activity

There were not many non-governmental organisations (NGOs) working directly on trafficking. However, the research team was able to collaborate with four organisations for the purpose of collecting data and in the analysis of service-delivery to trafficked persons. The operations of NGOs can be divided into four main areas of work designed to resist trafficking and child prostitution.

Social programmes: These include making available emergency shelter for victims of trafficking, counselling, health care education and some vocational training. Each NGO has a particular target group and a specific way of working: the Centre for the Protection of Children's Rights, for example, provides assistance, shelter and rehabilitation to abused children under 18. The religious-based groups focus on services to women who have been arrested or trafficked, but are rarely in a position to do much about the underlying factors which contribute towards trafficking.

Legal programmes: Some agencies provided legal advice and assistance during court hearings and proceedings. The overall level of expertise was not high, and there was not a great deal of interest in using the law to combat trafficking or to seek compensation for its victims. The difficulties in this respect were exacerbated by the indifference of law enforcers, and inadequate protection of the privacy of witnesses and victims.

Disseminating information: Part of each NGO's purpose was to bring home to the public the scale and extent of trafficking and prostitution. The most effective work through the media was accomplished in co-operative ventures between governmental and non-governmental agencies. Great care had to be taken to ensure that the women involved were not placed in further jeopardy by publicising their real-life stories.

NGOs and the international dimension: To dismantle international trafficking networks, co-operation between NGOs across national boundaries is required. Campaigns to change government policies and to provide effective help for trafficked persons must be co-ordinated by popular movements and NGOs in both sending and receiving countries. Such collaboration has worked well in tracing missing persons, in the joint provision of social and legal assistance in both the country of residence and the country of origin, and in media campaigns to inform the public. One good example of this has been the co-operation between NGOs in Japan and in Thailand to plead for leniency in the Shimodate case. The obstacles to such international efforts include language difficulties and cultural differences in ways of looking at and dealing with the issue. Some organisations underestimate the capacity of the women themselves to act on their own behalf.

Co-operation to combat trafficking

Powerful national and international strategies are needed to combat international trafficking. At present the level of co-operation between agencies within countries and between countries is inadequate.

Between government departments: The researchers found evidence of duplication between departments in their efforts to counter child prostitution. Co-operation between representatives of different departments was more effective in implementing the law which deals with the detention and 'rehabilitation' of sex workers. This has little impact on the sex industry itself. When it came to the Department of Public Welfare and the Ministry of Foreign Affairs working together to check applications for passports, this proved to be an unsuccessful tactic to discover whether trafficking was involved. The Public Welfare Department had instructions to check the background of young Thai women who applied for passports, to ensure that traffickers were not involved. The Foreign Affairs Ministry, however, refused to pass on information about applicants, on the grounds that it might be accused of unnecessary interference and discrimination.

The best examples of co-operation between governments are to be found in the detention and repatriation of illegal immigrants. The police officer interviewed in Malaysia by the project researcher stressed the co-operation with the Thai branch of Interpol in providing interpreters for cases against migrant sex workers. The Thai government, however, exhibited little interest in the plight of Thai women forced into prostitution overseas. During one case in Germany, in which defendants were prosecuted for forced prostitution, requests to the Thai police for witnesses were refused (Rayanakorn 1995).

Between government and NGOs: The response to the issue and to the women themselves is a source of conflict between government and non-governmental agencies. During the second phase of the research, the team was supporting a witness for a prosecution in Germany. They sought the compliance of the Thai police department. The police later released the information, including the identity of the victim, to the local press. They continued to defend their action, even though this threatens further collaboration between them and the Foundation for Women.

There were, however, examples of effective co-operation. The Thai Embassy in Tokyo is responsive to Japanese NGOs in bringing assistance to Thai women in distress. The Thai Ministry of Labour and Social Welfare and the Ministry of Foreign Affairs have provided some financial support to these Japanese NGOs.

Between NGOs: Transnational co-operation between NGOs in providing material help to individual women is well established. This is impaired to some degree by agencies supplying inadequate background information to cases that they refer and failing to follow them up. Co-operation within the country is also limited. Where it occurs, it is mostly on the basis of individual cases, rather than in a concerted effort to lobby government on the particular legislative measures required to address the problems.

International organisations: In October 1994, the Foundation for Women, together with the VENA Centre of the University of Leiden, and the Women's Studies Centre of Chiang Mai University, organised an international workshop on migration and trafficking of women. Some 70 people from 22 countries took part. The event concluded with an action plan for international co-operation, and recommendations were drawn up for national and international policies.

The Global Alliance Against Traffic in Women (GAATW) was formed. Its function is to co-ordinate efforts across national boundaries to promote international law reform and the adoption and enforcement of laws to combat trafficking. Part of its mandate is also to spread information and to promote research. It has set up working groups in a number of countries, including a group for research and co-ordination at the Foundation for Women in Bangkok.

Conclusion

Evidence emerged from the second phase of the project of the ability of migrant women themselves, their families and communities, to take on the issue of trafficking. Governmental and non-governmental agencies can provide support and information to active groups rooted in village and community. Outside agencies can contribute by linking women's groups across the country, and by arranging fact-finding trips. The participation of women in discussions and decisions about trafficking and migration is vital at all levels, for it is their livelihood, their lives, and their freedoms that are at stake.

The research also identified gaps in co-operation between agencies, many of which derive from conflicting views on prostitution and women migrants. Efforts to eradicate trafficking can be made more difficult by negative attitudes towards sex workers. This not only leads to gratuitous humiliation of the women, but also undermines co-operation on the prosecution of traffickers.

At present, prostitution represents the most hopeful option for some women. This, in turn, raises other vital questions. Is it more useful to apply the law to improve their working conditions, or to seek to eliminate the whole industry? The distinction must be maintained between issues of trafficking and of prostitution. Where prostitution is forced by coercion or violence, the law must be deployed against recruiters, brokers, agents and employers, and all those who collude with this damaging and degrading trade.

10

Conclusion

Traffic in women and forced prostitution are dehumanising and criminal acts, and represent serious violations of human rights. The trafficking of women generates huge profits for those involved in it, and exposes them to fewer risks than trade in other illegal goods – arms, drugs or endangered species of animals and plants. Law enforcement is inadequate, both nationally and internationally, because of a general perception that trafficked women, especially prostitutes, migrate of their own free will and allow themselves to be sold. This indifference to the trade can only encourage its growth and expansion. The international networks give rise not only to South–North migration, but also to migration between countries in the South. There are countries which are at the same time countries of origin, destination and transit for trafficked persons.

The trade in human beings is an outcrop of international labour migration, and cannot be separated from it. Millions of people seek to migrate temporarily to work in richer countries in order to improve their economic standing at home. For men, in spite of the closing of borders in Europe and North America, opportunities still exist. For women migrants, apart from domestic labour (itself often subject to conditions of virtual captivity), prostitution is one of the few options. The traffickers, with their extensive networks, move in on the voluntary movement of women, and divert them into forced labour.

The forces that make possible the traffic in women are visible at all levels. Inequality between countries is reflected in growing inequality within almost every country on earth. The sexual division of labour and unequal opportunities for women only serve the vast unofficial market that trades in human beings.

Poverty alone does not, however, offer a full explanation for migration and trafficking of women. By observing the situation at the local level, we come to a fuller understanding of how women who desire to migrate fall into the clutches of the traffickers. A decision to migrate, rarely taken lightly, usually arises when individuals or families see no way of improving their lives other than leaving their homes. They also have confidence in their ability to deal with the uncertainties and consequences of migration (Sripraphai and Sripraphai 1994). It is when that right to decide for themselves is usurped that migrants become vulnerable to the agents and employees of the human trade networks. They are susceptible to threats, deception and violence. Migrants then cease to be free, and that is when they need help and protection.

Power Relationships and the Trade in Human Beings

The trafficking of migrants is a world-wide phenomenon, and takes many forms. Migrant labourers become slave labour; illegal migrants are subject to blackmail, extortion and fear of exposure, often captives in closed and clandestine work-sites. Women migrants who may have departed with the intention of doing industrial or domestic work are frequently coerced into prostitution or sexual service. Some who migrate for marriage find themselves the objects of exploitation and abuse without limit. Their illegal status prevents them from seeking redress; their unfamiliarity with the language of the country depowers them, and exposes them to torments that only now are being told.

No one has been able to calculate how many, among the 70 million international migrants in the world, are victims of trafficking (Archavanitkul 1995: 2). The International Organisation for Migration estimates that world-wide the figure reaches several hundred thousand. These generate billions of dollars of profit for the traffickers (IOM 1994). Women run a far higher risk than men of being trafficked; the lack of employment choices for women, and high demand in the international sex trade, are obvious contributory factors. The trafficking in persons is rooted in unequal power relations between rich and poor and between men and women, a situation which the single global economy is not designed to reverse. Traffic in women is not confined to prostitution, and the definition of such traffic should not be limited to prostitution – forced industrial labour and mail-order brides are equally victims.

The trafficking network

Typically, and contrary to public perception, migrants are rarely the poorest in their community. They have to be able to afford the cost of migration, and must have something to sell or mortgage – land, property, cattle. However, in relation to other households, from which family members have already migrated for work, and which are receiving remittances from abroad, people may have a strong subjective feeling of disadvantage. The findings of the research provide evidence that many people are exploited by local recruiting agents, often respected members of the community, who have connections extending from nearby urban areas to foreign countries. In this way, hopeful migrant workers are easily caught up in an invisible web of criminal networks designed to exploit their ambitions for self-improvement. The relationship between trafficker and victim is not only one of master and slave, but also evolves into that of patron and client. The patron–client element develops once the trafficked person begins to send money home, and the family feels indebted to those who have procured or deceived their daughters. For the trafficked individual, the relationship becomes one of dependency for personal security, and for the return home.

As well as conveying women from their villages to the destination, the traffickers are always on the lookout for new routes and new destinations. Germany, for example, became a receiving country for Thai women in the 1980s, and remains one. It is estimated that in Berlin alone there as many as 5,000 Thai women who are forced sex workers (Ban Ying 1994). Over time, exploitation has been intensified, working conditions have deteriorated and wages decreased. The price of service from women sex workers has fallen from DM300 to DM200, as a result of increased competition among migrant prostitutes. Women are being sold on to other clubs and bars, their debts are escalating, and they depend on their employers for visas. Some have had to pay men for false marriage documents to ensure that they can stay in the country.

Family and migration

The research found that returned migrant women who maintain contacts in the countries of destination are often instrumental in persuading others to migrate. There was also evidence that some families recruit for prostitution among their own members. The ties of kinship complicate the situation. People are more trusting of their relatives, however distant. This also deters them from taking legal action against agents. In their view of obligation to family, there is clearly a difference between traffickers and migrants: the traffickers have no concern about the relative they may be trafficking, but the victims and their families will hesitate before they harm the trafficker who wields such power over them.

Women as victims?

Women's limited choices render them more vulnerable to trafficking, and they are liable to be victimised in a number of ways. They may be deceived about the nature of the work they are undertaking; they may be unaware of working conditions; they may not even know their destination. They may travel on false documents, overstay their visas, work in illegal venues, risk arrest and detention. Their work may be unpaid or underpaid because of inflated debts to agents and employers. There is pressure from their families to remit money. This all creates a high degree of stress, and they may seek relief through drugs or gambling.

In spite of this, migrant women try to make the best of their situation. Their capacity for endurance, their tenacity and stoicism often remain concealed and uncelebrated, unknown to their loved ones, unseen by their indifferent manipulators. Some do escape, others work longer and harder, some seek to sustain illusions about their lives, at least when talking to family and friends. They want to preserve the reputation of dutiful daughter or wife providing for the family, even if this is at the cost of their integrity or safety. The maintenance of this image that all is well serves to perpetuate the stream of international migration, inspiring rather than deterring others.

Change in the family and community

Migration, forced prostitution and traffic in women are bound to have serious repercussions on both family and community. They modify the structure of families. The bonds between husband and wife or parents and children can be stretched by long absences. In some cases, the destiny and decisions of individual women are controlled not by the family, but by anonymous members of migration and trafficking networks. The transfer of responsibility from parents to outsiders – agents and employers – creates new ties between family and agents.

Children of migrant workers are deeply marked by the absence of parents. Some are subject to ridicule when it becomes known that their mothers are working as prostitutes. Teenagers in particular appear to find it most problematical in adjusting to the absence of parents or the taunts of others. There are few sources of help for the children of migrants.

Whole communities are affected by migration and trafficking. Families of women forced into prostitution often deploy conspicuous wealth to counter criticism and to buy respect from neighbours. Traditional generosity between households is undermined by competitiveness and moral judgements.

The impact of traffic in women upon receiving countries is rarely examined. What happens to families whose husbands and fathers financially support second wives, and who visit them for significant periods? What effect does the presence of trafficking networks and criminal syndicates have upon the people's attitude towards prostitutes and migrant women in general? In Japan, for example, publicity was given to allegations that foreign sex workers were spreading AIDS, and people were encouraged to report their presence to the police. Further exploration of these issues will also help to define ways to combat trafficking which do not lead to further discrimination against migrants and trafficked persons.

The Role of Governments

The governments of countries of origin, destination and transit have made little progress in eradicating the traffic in women. Action has too often been directed at punishing the victims rather than the traffickers. Immigration laws are invoked to prosecute the women, and policies to provide social support for victims have not yet been formulated. If migration is made more difficult, this only serves to intensify the dependency of women on agents and exploiters.

Most receiving and sending countries have no clear policy and no coherent plan on trafficking. Where prostitution is legal, governments tend to show more concern about trafficking. In countries where it is illegal, the courts are more concerned about the illegality of the woman's work or status than they are about the circumstances that drove her to seek such work. Anti-prostitution laws may even work in favour of traffickers, because there is more money to be made from it, and they have no responsibility for repatriating the women if they are arrested. A strengthening of laws against trafficking would have the effect of promoting understanding of and sympathy for trafficked persons.

Violation of human rights

An examination of the mechanisms employed by traffickers to deceive and coerce women is vital to an understanding of the traffic in women. These mechanisms constitute a violation of human rights. International conventions against slavery, trafficking, and the rights of migrants and the rights of women can all be invoked to publicise abuses of these conventions, and to draw attention to government neglect of its commitments. Existing laws should be used to persuade governments to take more responsibility for and to provide more help to victims.

Many factors conspire to make effective action against trafficking extremely difficult. The collusive dependency that is often set up between families who derive economic 'benefit' from their daughters' absence and those who traffic them is one element. The secretive – because illegal – way of life of the women in foreign countries, trapped by employers who share a vested interest in concealment is another. Governments whose women are trafficked have no wish for adverse publicity, and this may make them hesitate to uncover the extent of the trade. Similarly, it is scarcely to the credit of countries of destination to advertise the fact that their nationals routinely abuse, exploit and employ the sexual services of captive foreign women.

The traffic in women starkly illuminates the nature of the global market economy; its very illegality casts an oblique light on the mechanisms which are now the object of universal acceptance – the sanctification of the market as the supreme means of answering human need. In many ways, women are the perfect commodity. Demand exists; the supply follows to those places where demand is highest. Great ingenuity and enterprise are deployed in uniting customers with their requirements. Much wealth is created. Employment is generated. The fact that the objects of this marketing are living, breathing flesh and blood and not articles of manufacture is a matter of indifference to the impersonal mechanisms of the market. If ever there were an argument against relying upon the market as the arbiter of our destiny, this, surely, is it.

What all this means is that pressure must be maintained by the people, both on governments and international bodies, to take the initiative in pursuing and putting an end to this cruel form of merchandising, this modernised version of slavery, this ancient and squalid trade in human persons.

Recommendations

These recommendations are not specific to Thailand, but are equally valid for any organisation in countries where trafficking is a matter of concern.

Local level

Centres for advice on migration and for counselling potential migrants should be established under the control of local people in districts from which there is a high rate of out-migration.

In addition to providing general information, such centres can offer legal advice to returned migrants, and support in pursuing cases against brokers and traffickers.

Sub-district and district councils should include the issues of migration and trafficking in their plans for action.

Women, especially those with experience of migration and trafficking, should be well represented in decision-making at local level when policies and actions are formulated.

Core groups of villagers to work on issues of migration and trafficking should be encouraged. Members should be trained in techniques of informing and assisting others in the village.

Special attention should be given to providing skills to young people, so that they can find good employment locally.

Non-formal education programmes should include information on the risks and dangers of migration and trafficking.

People planning to migrate for work should be informed of their rights, under national and international laws and agreements.

A local programme should be set up to help returned trafficked workers. This could include a support group of those with similar experiences abroad, and familiar with problems of readjustment.

Efforts should be made in all education and information programmes to break down the distinction between 'good' and 'bad' women, to make it easier for returned sex workers to re-integrate into the community.

National level

General government activity: A national programme should be formulated to combat domestic and international trafficking. In devising this programme, governments should consult NGOs with expertise in this field.

As a basis for policy-making, further research should be funded to assess the scale and extent of trafficking in women.

National standards should be laid down for the treatment of trafficked persons.

Governments should collaborate with NGOs and other governments in the exchange of information and to facilitate the return of trafficked women. This will create an effective network to combat trafficking.

Governments should set up a national office for co-ordinating work on this issue, or assign the work to an existing one.

Governments should grant nationality rights to minority groups which have lived for several generations within its borders. This will address the problem of statelessness of some migrant workers.

In the light of research on trafficking, national policies on the export of labour and migration should be reviewed, so that these do not further the objectives of traffickers.

Law and law enforcement: Laws relating to trafficking should be reviewed, to ensure that they are effective in the protection of trafficked women, especially when the women are involved in legal proceedings over a trafficking offence.

Before existing legislation is reviewed or fresh anti-trafficking laws are drafted, wide public consultation should take place.

When it comes to prosecutions, courts should focus on the crime of trafficking, not on the 'moral' behaviour of the victims. A woman's previous work should be irrelevant, and her testimony must be given a weight equal to that of other witnesses.

Prostitution should be decriminalised for two reasons: to minimise the power and control of criminal syndicates; to reduce the social stigma of sex work.

The enforcement of labour laws should be extended so that they cover places of entertainment and prostitution.

The anti-trafficking law should allow for the confiscation of assets of those found guilty of trafficking; part of which should go as compensation to the trafficked persons, and part to fund anti-trafficking campaigns.

An independent human rights body should be set up to monitor the activities of law enforcement agencies. This body should have the power to recommend prosecution where human rights violations have occurred.

There should be a specific police unit to deal with the issue of violence against women. Within the unit, there should be a section concerned with trafficking. It should be given sufficient resources to fulfil its functions, and officers should be specially trained.

An exchange programme between police forces in different countries who deal with trafficking should be encouraged. This will make for better co-operation and sharing of information in the detection and prosecution of traffickers. Anti-trafficking units should contain a number of officers with English-language skills, to facilitate international co-operation.

In interviews and court proceedings, the trafficked women should be protected against further intimidation or reprisals. The following steps should be taken wherever possible:

• Interviews conducted in private, and court testimony given in closed court;

- the woman's identity suppressed from public knowledge;
- women police officers to conduct all interviews;
- interviewers to have a high level of training in dealing with violence against women in general, and trafficking in particular;
- a support person for the woman to be present at all times;
- liaison with relevant outside agencies to assist the woman;
- cases processed quickly;
- all documents explained in full to the woman.

Employment: Appropriate vocational training should be provided for women vulnerable to trafficking and for returned migration.

Employment opportunities should be offered to returned trafficked women who are HIV-positive as a consequence of prostitution.

General educational programmes should be modified, to emphasise the positive role of the girl child, and to raise the self-esteem of girls in schools.

There should be financial support from the government to enable girls from poorer backgrounds to continue their education.

Returned migrants should be given opportunities for further education.

The curriculum of state education should include issues specific to women, and give prominence to violence against women.

The government should undertake public education on the risks of migration for work; and this should be supported by the mass media.

Health and social services: Effective health services should be provided for trafficked persons, particularly for those who prove to be HIV-positive.

Mandatory HIV testing of trafficked women should be forbidden. Where testing has been required by the woman, the results should remain confidential.

A woman doctor should conduct all physical examinations required for evidence in criminal proceedings.

An emergency refuge for trafficked women should be set up, so that when they return, they can remain for a time in a congenial atmosphere, and be protected from media and other public scrutiny.

Returned trafficked women should be provided with the financial means to rebuild their lives.

Information: Information centres should be set up to provide advice and assistance in such practical matters as passport applications, dealing with foreign embassies or national embassies overseas.

Such centres should help with reports of missing persons, and pursue enquiries with the relevant agencies and departments, both within the country and abroad.

Such centres should call upon the resources of people with local knowledge of trafficking networks.

A national co-ordinating office should provide help to these information centres, and should issue material for public distribution on topics such as emergency help, visa applications, passports and embassy contacts.

Non-governmental sector: NGOs should co-operate with government in drawing up national policies on trafficking, the proper treatment of trafficked persons and plans of action.

NGOs should unite as necessary to lobby the government to act on trafficking.

NGOs should co-operate across national borders to ensure that work against trafficking is effective, and that assistance to trafficked persons reaches them. This co-operation could include individual casework, seminars for the exchange of information and data, joint research and agreement on the services to be provided by each organisation involved.

NGOs should make contact with their embassies overseas for a continuous exchange of information and for co-operation on individual cases.

In order to avoid duplication of effort, a co-ordinating body of NGOs should be formed to oversee the work to combat trafficking and to assist trafficked persons.

NGOs should encourage the formation of rural networks of returned migrant women and those involved in the fight against trafficking.

In co-operation with the government, information should be produced for the media in order to launch a campaign against trafficking.

Co-operation with institutions of higher education should modify curricula and promote joint research programmes.

NGOs should try to follow up cases of all returned trafficked women to ensure that all the assistance they require has been provided.

Accurate documentation of all cases should be made for use in lobbying for policy change at national and international levels.

NGOs should organise trips that will enable community workers and NGO personnel to see for themselves the conditions in which migrant workers live, and to exchange ideas for action with other community groups.

Mass Media: Journalists concerned with trafficking issues should report on the violations of human rights, and at the same time respect these rights by not revealing the identity of victims.

An appropriate code of conduct should be adopted by journalists dealing with victims of crime.

Joint seminars between media personnel, government and NGO officers
should be held, for an exchange of information and to devise ways
of co-operating effectively.

Regional level

A regional plan of action to combat trafficking is needed. This would
facilitate communications and expose regional patterns of trafficking.
The training of government and NGO personnel should be co-
ordinated.
Major regional forums, such as ASEAN, should address the issue.
Multilateral agreements between countries in the region should aim to
bring swift assistance to trafficked persons and to prosecute
offenders.

International level

The existing international instruments relating to the traffic in persons
should be reviewed, to determine their effectiveness in the
contemporary context. In particular, the 1949 UN Convention for
the Suppression of the Traffic in Persons and of the Exploitation
of the Prostitution of Others is in urgent need of review.
A thematic UN special rapporteur should be appointed to deal with the
issue of trafficking: the mandate for the rapporteur on violence
against women is too wide to accommodate the issue adequately.
Global plans of action on combating the traffic in women should be
adopted.
Standard minimum rules for the treatment of trafficked persons should
be developed and acted upon.
Undocumented workers should be entitled to the same protection
extended to other migrant workers under all International Labour
Organisation agreements.
The UN and national governments should apply pressure to countries
through which trafficking routes pass so that they adopt anti-
trafficking laws and policies.
The UN should launch an international year and decade to end
trafficking in women.
The UN or other international bodies should provide funds for
organisations which document cases and pursue complaints of
human rights violations at the international level.
International agencies should collaborate with national agencies to
organise training in law, literacy and human rights for people active
in the struggle against trafficking.

Member states of the UN should apply international pressure on those states which do not protect the rights of trafficked persons, or in which such rights have been violated.

The effect of global factors on trafficking, particularly economic factors, should be investigated, as should the consequences of international actions, such as the operations of UN peacekeeping forces.

International pressure should be applied to countries which take repressive action against the victims of trafficking.

Interpol should compile a list of known traffickers and should vigorously pursue and prosecute them across national borders.

Multilateral agreements for the extradition of criminals and for ensuring the safety and repatriation of trafficked persons should be drawn up.

Appendix

Draft of standard minimum rules for the treatment of victims of trafficking in persons and forced labour and slavery-like practices

Drafted by the Global Alliance Against Traffic in Women and The Foundation For Women, in co-operation with the Foundation Against Trafficking in Women.

The following Standards aim to protect the human rights of those individuals who have been victim of trafficking in persons and related forced labour and slavery-like practices, in particular the right to control over one's mind, body and life.[1]

Keeping in mind that victims of trafficking and the related forced labour and slavery-like practices are not criminals but victims of crime, governments should take all necessary steps to reform any law or policy that punishes, criminalises or marginalises the victims of these practices and to ensure them the humane treatment stated below.

Recognising that traffickers exploit poverty, gender violence, armed conflicts, and other conditions which subordinate persons and which they may seek to escape, protection must be given to individuals in situations which render them vulnerable to deception as well as physical, psychological and economic coercion and violence.

Governments should take all necessary steps to ensure victims of trafficking and forced labour and slavery-like practices the equal protection of the law and to guarantee them the rights and fundamental freedoms of all individuals, including the freedom of movement and residence in each State, the freedom to choose one's place of residence, the right to safely return to one's own country, and the right to seek asylum or otherwise legalise one's status in the country of destination.

Definitions

Trafficking in persons

All acts involved in the recruitment and/or transportation of a person within and across national borders for work or services by means of violence or threat of violence, abuse of authority or dominant position, debt-bondage, deception or other forms of coercion.

Forced labour and slavery-like practices

The extraction of work or services from any person or the appropriation of the legal identity and/or physical person of any person by means of violence or threat of violence, abuse of authority or dominant position, debt-bondage, deception or other forms of coercion.

Background of the definitions

The above formulated definitions go back to two international agreements: the League of Nations Slavery Convention of 1926 and the Supplementary Convention of 1956[2] which condemn all slavery-like practices, including debt-bondage[3] and forced marriage[4] and the ILO Forced Labour Convention no. 29.[5] These conventions have broad international acceptance and clearly describe the situations at hand. In the Slavery Convention the concept of 'ownership' is fundamental to slavery, which in article 1.1 is defined as: 'the status or condition of a person over whom any or all of the power attaching to the right of ownership are exercised'.

In article 2 of the ILO Forced Labour Convention, forced or compulsory labour is defined as: 'all work or service which is extracted from any person under the menace of any penalty and for which the said person has not offered himself voluntarily'.

Whereas the concept of 'forced labour' in article 1 of the ILO Convention is predominantly used for the relation between the state and the individual, article 4.1 of the same Convention rules on state accountability regarding forced labour situations between individuals: 'the competent authority shall not impose or permit the imposition of forced or compulsory labour for the benefit of private individuals, companies or associations'.

The crucial element in both definitions is coercion, which can take various forms, including but not limited to:

- violence or threat of violence, including deprivation of freedom (of movement, of personal choice)
- deception with regard to working conditions or the nature of the work to be done
- abuse of authority, dominant position; this can range from confiscation of personal documents to place another person in a dependent position, abusing one's dominant social position, abusing one's natural parental authority or abusing the vulnerable position of persons without legal status
- debt-bondage: pledging the personal services or labour of a person indefinitely as security for a debt, when the length and nature of the service is not clearly defined.

Work or services include all domestic, sexual, reproductive or other services rendered under the above-mentioned conditions of coercion, regardless of whether these services are recognised as work, whether they take place under a work contract or whether they take place under a marriage contract.

The appropriation of the legal identity and/or physical person refers to the concept of partial or total ownership as used in the Slavery Conventions, but the word 'appropriation' is used to denote the act of claiming ownership of a person, acting as if one owns the person.

Appropriation of the legal identity can range from confiscating one's identity papers, supplying a person with a false identity to the loss of one's legal personality under the marriage contract.

Country of origin: the country of origin of the trafficked person.

Country of destination: the country of destination of the trafficked person.

Transit country: the country *en route* from the country of origin to the country of destination, often for the purpose of preparing false passports, marriage documents, visas.

Obligations of All Countries:
Destinations, Transit and Origins

1.   The following shall be guaranteed to all victims of trafficking and forced labour and slavery-like practices:

a)   Freedom from persecution or harassment by those in positions of authority.

b)   Adequate, confidential and affordable medical and psychological care by the State or, if no adequate State agency exists, by a private agency funded by the State.

c)   Strictly confidential HIV testing service shall be provided ONLY

IF requested by the person concerned. Additionally, any and all HIV testing must be accompanied with appropriate pre- and post-test counselling. The Standard provided in the UN Centre for Human Rights and World Health Organisation Report of an International Consultation on AIDS and Human Rights, Geneva, July 1989 shall be adopted.

d) Access to a competent, qualified translator during all proceedings, and provision of all documents and records pursuant to having been victim of trafficking and/or forced labour and slavery-like practices.[6]

e) Free legal assistance.

f) Legal possibilities of compensation and redress for economic, physical and psychological damage caused to them.

g) The personal history, the alleged 'character' or the current or previous occupation of the victim shall not be used against the victim, nor serve as a reason to disqualify the victim's complaint or to decide not to prosecute the offenders. The offenders cannot use as a defence the fact that the person is or was at any time, for example, a prostitute or a domestic worker.

h) The victim's history of being trafficked and/or being subjected to forced labour and slavery-like practices shall not be a matter of public or private record and shall not be used against her, her family or friends in any way whatsoever, particularly with regard to the right to freedom of travel, marriage, search for gainful employment.

2. The State in the territory under whose jurisdiction the trafficking and/or forced labour and slavery-like practices took place shall take all necessary steps to ensure that the victim, if he or she wishes so, may press criminal charges and/or take civil action for compensation against the perpetrator(s).[7]

3. If the victim is not recognised as citizen by the country of origin for any reason, the country of origin must consider on the balance of probabilities whether that person was born in and/or has spent most of her/his life in the country of origin and if so, accord that person nationality of the country of origin. If the country of origin will not accept the victim, the country of destination must treat her as a national of that country under the Convention on the Status of Stateless Persons (1960).

4. The State must ensure the right of all people within its jurisdiction to be free from being sold by any other person[8] and/or from being subjected to forced labour and slavery-like practices in accordance with the ILO Convention no. 29 concerning Forced Labour, article 1.4.1.

Obligations of Destination and Transit Countries

5.   In addition to the above, and in order to ensure the victim's ability to remain in the country during all proceedings pursuant to having been victim of trafficking and/or forced labour and slavery-like practices, the victim shall, for the duration of her stay, be guaranteed:

a)   resident status, in order to take legal action against the offenders and to regain control over her life

b)   adequate and safe housing

c)   ' access to all State provided health and social services

d)   adequate financial support

e)   opportunities for employment, education and training.

6.   Victims of trafficking and/or forced and slavery-like practices shall not be held in a detention centre at any time, including during proceedings against the offenders.

7.   Victims of trafficking and/or forced labour and slavery-like practices shall have access to the embassy/consulate of their home country or, if trafficked into a country without an embassy/consulate representation, they shall have access to a diplomatic representative of the State that takes charge of the home country's interests or any national or international authority whose task it is to protect such persons.[9]

8.   Victims of trafficking and/or forced labour and slavery-like practices shall not be prosecuted for the use of false travel or other documents and/or visas pursuant to their predicament.

9.   Victims who wish to do so, shall be enabled to apply for permanent residence under internationally agreed upon covenants. Guidelines recognising gender-based persecution as grounds for asylum should be followed.

10.   Victims of trafficking and/or forced labour and slavery-like practices shall be guaranteed the right to legal representation during criminal or other proceedings against her or him that may result in detention, deportation or loss of legal status. If she cannot afford to pay, legal representation shall be provided without cost.[10]

11.   The burden of proof prior to and during any prosecution of a person alleged to be guilty of trafficking and/or forced labour and slavery-like practices lies with the prosecution, not with the victim. The victims shall not be placed in detention prior to the trial of the offender.

12.   If a person is convicted of trafficking and/or subjecting another person to forced labour and slavery-like practices, any or all funds in his/her possession shall be used to pay any debts the victim incurred as a consequence of being trafficked and/or subjected to forced labour and slavery-like practices. Additionally, adequate compensation shall be granted to the victim.

13. The State shall provide the necessary funds for the victim to return to her/his home country.

14. If a victim of trafficking and/or forced labour and slavery-like practices person is arrested under the criminal law of the country for committing a crime:

a) As a result of physical, psychological or economic duress or coercion by the person(s) who trafficked her and/or subjected her to forced labour and slavery-like practices: these circumstances shall be considered in any defence of duress or coercion raised by the victim during the pre-trial and trial proceedings and as mitigation in sentencing if convicted.

b) Against the person who trafficked her and/or subjected her to forced labour and slavery-like practices, including homicide.

c) The history of trafficking and/or being subjected to forced labour and slavery-like practices shall be permitted in support of a plea of self-defence and as a mitigation during sentencing if convicted.

Obligations of Countries of Origin

15. Victims of forced labour and slavery-like practices who return to their home country shall not be imprisoned or detained for facts pursuant to their predicament, nor for the use of false travel and other documents.

16. The State shall protect victims of trafficking and/or forced labour and slavery-like practices and their family members from reprisals of the perpetrators, including people in positions of authority.

17. The State shall not do anything to prevent or obstruct the voluntary movement of citizens, including victims of trafficking and/or forced labour and slavery-like practices, out or into the country at all times.[11]

18. The State shall use diplomatic channels and resources in destination and transit countries to protect their nationals abroad.

Notes

1. See also International Covenant on Civil and Political Rights (ICCPR), articles 1 and 8; Protection of the Rights of All Migrant Workers, 1990, article 16 paragraphs 1 and 2: Slavery Convention, 1926; Supplementary Convention on the Abolition of Slavery, the Slave Trade, and Institutions and Practices Similar to Slavery 1956. Preamble ('Considering that freedom is the birthright of every human being') and article 1.

2. Slavery Convention, 1926; Supplementary Convention on the

Abolition of Slavery, the Slave Trade, and Institutions and Practices similar to Slavery, 1956.

3. Article 1a of the Supplementary Slavery Convention prohibits 'Debt bondage, that is to say, the status or condition arising from a pledge by a debtor of his personal services or those of a person under his control as security for a debt, if the value of those services as reasonably assessed is not applied towards the liquidation of the debt or the length and nature of those services are not respectively limited and defined'.

4. Article 1c of the Supplementary Slavery Convention prohibits 'Any institution or practice whereby a woman without the right to refuse, is promised or given in marriage on payment of a consideration in money or kind to her parents, guardian, family or any other person or group', or whereby 'the husband of a woman, his family, or his clan, has the right to transfer her to another person for value received or otherwise'.

5. ILO Convention no. 29 concerning Forced Labour, 1930.

6. See also Protection of the Rights of all Migrant Workers, article 16, paragraph 5.

7. See International Covenant on Civil and Political Rights, article 2.3.

8. See Supplementary Convention on the Abolition of Slavery, the Slave Trade, and Institutions and Practices Similar to Slavery, 1956, article 1, paragraph C, sub-paragraphs i–iii.

9. See 38 (2) of the Standard Minimum Rules For the Treatment of Prisoners 1955.

10. See ICCPR, article 14.3; Protection of all Persons under any Form of Detention, Principle 17, paragraphs 1 and 2; Principle 18, paragraphs 1–5.

11. See Universal Declaration of Human Rights, article 13; ICCPR, article 12.

Bibliography

In English:

Advies Commissie Mensenrechten (1986) *Crossing Borders: The Right to Leave a Country and the Right to Return*, Report No. 3, The Hague.

Archavaniktul, K. (1993) 'Female Migration and Traffic in Women from Thailand', unpublished paper presented at National Workshop on the Research and Action Project on Traffic in Women of the Foundation for Women, Bangkok, 29 July 1993.

—— and P. Guest (1993) 'Migration and the Commercial Sex Sector in Thailand', paper prepared for Seminar on AIDS Impact and Prevention in the Developing World: the Contribution of Demography and Social Science, France, 5–9 December 1993.

Asia Watch, Women's Rights Project (1994) *A Modern Form of Slavery: Trafficking of Burmese Women and Girls into Brothels in Thailand*, New York: Human Rights Watch.

Ban Ying (1994) *The Traffic in Foreign Women in Berlin: A Description of the Present Situation*, Berlin: Ban Ying Coordination Center.

Boonchalaksi, W. and P. Guest (1994) *Prostitution in Thailand*, Publication No. 171, Bangkok: Mahidoi University, Institute for Population and Social Research.

Brummelhuis, H. ten (1984) 'Abundance and Avoidance: An Interpretation of Thai Individualism', in H. ten Brummelhuis and J. H. Kemp (eds), *Strategies and Structures in Thai Society*, Publication series ZZOA, No. 31, ASC, Amsterdam: University of Amsterdam.

Chant, S. (1992) 'Toward a framework for the analysis of gender selective migration', in S. Chant (ed.), *Gender and Migration in Developing Countries*, London: Belhaven Press.

—— and S. Radcliffe (1992) 'Migration and development: the importance of gender', in S. Chant (ed.), *Gender and Migration in Developing Countries*, London: Belhaven Press.

Chantavanich, S. (1995) 'Crossborder Migration in Asia-Pacific and Labour Linkages', unpublished paper, Asian Research Centre for Migration, Institute of Asian Studies, Chulalongkorn University, Bangkok.

The Traffic in Women

Hartl, M. (1995) 'Traffic in Women as a Form of Violence against Women', in Klap et al. (eds) (1995).

Heyzer, N. (1986) *Working Women in South East Asia: Development, Subordination and Emancipation*, Philadelphia, Milton Keynes: Open University Press.

IOM (International Organization for Migration) (1994) 'Trafficking in Migrants: Characteristics and Trends in Different Regions of the World', discussion paper presented to the International Conference on Transnational Migration in the Asia–Pacific Region: Problems and Prospects, Institute of Asia Studies, Chulalongkorn University, Bangkok, 1–2 December 1994.

Karp, J. (1995) 'A New Kind of Hero', *Far Eastern Economic Review* 30 (30), 1995.

Klap, Marieke, et al. (eds) (1995) *Combating Traffic in Persons: Conclusions of the Conference on Traffic in Persons*, Utrecht/Maastricht: University of Utrecht, Department of the Law of International Organizations.

Mansson, SA. (1995) 'International Prostitution and Traffic in Persons from a Swedish Perspective', in Klap et al. (eds) (1995).

Massey, D. S. et al. (1993) 'Theories of International Migration: A Review and Appraisal', in *Population and Development Review*, Vol. 19, No. 3, September, 1993.

Macmahon, A. (1994) 'Trafficking and Forced Prostitution of Burmese Women in Thailand', unpublished paper, CPCR, Bangkok.

Pongsapich, A. (1994) 'International Migrant Workers in Asia: The Case of Thailand', paper presented to the International Conference on Transnational Migration in the Asia–Pacific Region: Problems and Prospects, Institutes of Asia Studies, Chulalongkorn University, Bangkok, 1–2 December 1994.

Potter, Jack M. (1976) *Thai Peasant Social Structure*, Chicago: The University of Chicago Press.

Rayanakorn, K. (1993) *Study of the Law Relating to Prostitution and Traffic in Women*, Bangkok: Foundation For Women.

Rosario, V. O. (1994) 'Lifting the Smoke Screen: Dynamics of Mail Order Bride Migration from the Philippines', unpublished PhD thesis, Institute of Social Studies, The Hague.

Sassen, S. (1994) 'Immigration in a World Economy', paper presented to the International Conference on Transnational Migration in the Asia–Pacific Region: Problems and Prospects, Institutes of Asia Studies, Chulalongkorn University, Bangkok, 1–2 December 1994.

Skrobanek, S. (1983) 'The Transnational Sexploitation of Thai Women', unpublished research paper, Women and Development Programme, Institute of Social Studies, The Hague.

—— (1993) 'Violence Against Women: Forms and Remedies', paper presented at the NGO Symposium for the Workshop on Violence against Women, Manila, 16–30 November 1993.

—— (1995) 'Law Relating to Traffic in Women: the Case of Thailand', in Klap et al. (eds) (1995).

Sripraphai, K. and P. Sripraphai (1984) 'Savan's Dilemma: An Analysis of Migration Decisions', in H. ten Brummelhuis and J. H. Kemp (eds), *Strategies and Structures in Thai Society*, Publication series ZZOA, No. 31, ASC, Amsterdam: University of Amsterdam.

Stalker, P. (1994) *The Work of Strangers: A Survey of International Labour Migration*, Geneva: International Labour Office.

van der Vleuten, N. (1991) *Survey on 'Traffic in Women': Policies and Policy Research in an International Context*, VENA Working Paper No. 91/1, Leiden: Research and Documentation Centre on Women and Autonomy.

Wijers, M. (1995) 'Supporting Victims of Trafficking', paper presented at the International Conference on Traffic in Persons, Utrecht/ Maastricht, 15–19 November 1994.

In Thai:

Bank of Thailand (1995) *Annual Report*, Bangkok.

Chivit Tong Suu (1994), interview with women, Yakuza, July.

Dararat Mettarikanondhu (1983) 'Government Policy on Prostitution in Thailand, 1868–1960', Master's thesis, Chulalongkorn University, Bangkok.

Foundation For Women (1989) *Mail Order Bride*, Bangkok: Women's Press.

Siam Post, 7 August 1995.

Thai Rath, 5 August 1995.

Index

Abatement of Prostitution Act, Thailand, 1, 8, 29, 32, 35, 69, 93
adoption, false, 18
agents/recruiters, 1, 33, 46, 51-4, 77-8, 81-2, 91, 100-1; fees, 88; international, 55
AIDS, 70-1, 102; related illness, 44
Archavanitkul, Kritaya, 15, 22-5, 55, 99
Asian Women's Human Rights Council, 81
Association of South East Asian Nations (ASEAN), 108
Australia, Thai sex workers, 47, 50

Ban Ying, 100
Bangkok, 1, 3, 33, 80; Chinese sex workers, 51; Emergency Home for Women, 9; Patpong District, 30-1, 35-9, 61; Suthisarn Street, 42-4
Bangladeshis, Sylhet, 15
beer bars, 61-2
Berlin, Ban Ying shelter, 46
bonded labour, 14, 16, 49, 58, 66
Brazil, 6
brothels, 1, 18, 42, 46, 57; closed, 56; Japanese, 64; open, 58; temple contributions, 78
Buddhist monks, 77-8
Burma, 34; sex workers, 50; Shan state, 1; women from, 17, 45

Canada, Thai sex workers, 50

cancer, cervical, 64
Caribbean, emigrants, 20
Centre for the Protection of Children's Rights, 94
Chant, S., 13, 15
Chiang Mai University, Women's Studies Centre, 96
Chiang Rai province, 1, 3, 10
children: of migrants, 101; prostitution, 77-8, 87, 92-5; relations to, 75; trafficking, 27
China, 34; labour migrants, 17, 29; Thai sex workers, 50; unofficial US emigration, 16; Yunan province, 51
Chuan Leekpai, 92
'comfort women', 17
community: attitudes, 82-5; changed values, 75-6; leaders' role, 77-8
condoms, 61
conspicuous consumption, 70, 74, 76, 92
Convention on the Elimination of All Forms of Discrimination Against Women (CEDAW), 27
crime syndicates, 16, 63-4, 84

debt, 49-50, 55-6, 58, 62, 64, 66, 68, 72, 81, 84, 88-9, 101
Denmark, mail-order brides, 65
division of labour: international, 9; sexual, 13, 98
divorce, rate, 75

The following pages contain a selection of Zed's recent and forthcoming titles - obtainable from all good bookshops.

Copies of all Zed Books and full catalogues may also be obtained from:

UK	Zed Books 7 Cynthia Street London NI 9JF Tel: 0171 837 4014 Fax: 0171 833 3960
USA	St Martin's Press Scholarly and Reference Division 175 Fifth Avenue New York NY 10010 Tel: (212) 982 3900 Fax: (212) 777 6359
Canada	Fernwood Books Ltd. PO Box 9409, Station 'A' Halifax, NS, B3K 5S3 Tel (902) 422 3302 Fax (902) 422 3179
Australia	Astam Books 57 - 61 John Street Leichhardt Sydney NSW 2040 (02) 9566 4400 (02) 9566 4411

WOMEN, POPULATION AND GLOBAL CRISIS
A Political-Economic Analysis
Asoka Bandarage, Mount Holyoke College

It has been widely assumed that over-population is one of the root causes of global crisis; even amongst feminist and environmental movements the common wisdom on population has never been seriously critiqued. This book provides that critique; it gives a historical overview of the population question and places the population-poverty-environment-security debate within a broad theoretical perspective.

'Placing the needs of women, and particularly women of color, at the centre of her analysis, Asoka Bandarage shows how the contradictions in the social and economic realities that dominate their lives jeopardize the well-being of us all. Her proposals for cooperative and democratic efforts to stem poverty give hope that we can build societies respectful of the needs of people and of the rest of the natural world.' – *Ruth Hubbard, Professor Emeritus of Biology, Harvard University*

Contents
Introduction
1. Malthusian Analysis of Global Crisis
2. Politics of Global Population Control
3. Historical Evolution of Socio-Demographic Relations
4. Social Structural Determinants of Fertility
5. Political Economy of Poverty
6. Political Economy of the Environment
7. Political Economy of Violence and Insecurity
8. Towards Psycho-Social Transformation

Women's Studies/Environment/Development
Hb 1 85649 427 6
Pb 1 85649 428 4
400pp Index Royal

WOMEN'S REBELLION AND ISLAMIC MEMORY
Fatima Mernissi
Author of *Beyond the Veil* and *The Forgotten Queens of Islam*

A collection of essays spanning over ten years of research, this book presents a sustained analysis of the position of women in the world of contemporary Islam. One of the most important feminist thinkers, Fatima Mernissi here makes a major contribution to the theorisation of gender roles and sexual identity in the Islamic world.

'Fatima Mernissi combines intellect with scholarship and a graceful style.' – *Sunday Times*

Contents
1. Writing is better than a face-lift
2. Building Baghdad in a different galaxy
3. Morocco: the merchant's daughter and the son of the Sultan
4. Women, saints and sanctuaries
5. Virginity and patriarchy
6. Is population control conceivable without democracy?
7. The conflict between the Islamic state and women
8. Women's work
9. The Jariya and the Caliph: reflections on the role of women in Muslim political memory
10. Women in Muslim history: traditional perspectives and new strategies
11. Femininity as subversion: reflections on the Muslim concept of Nushuz

Translated by Emily Agar

1996
Women's Studies/Middle East/Sociology
Hb 1 85649 397 0
Pb 1 85649 398 9
160pp Index Metric demy

THE WOMEN, GENDER AND DEVELOPMENT READER
Edited by Nalini Visvanathan (co-ordinator), Lynn Duggan, Laurie Nisonoff and Nan Wiegersma

Third World women were long the undervalued and ignored actors in the development process but are now recognized by scholars, practitioners and policy makers alike as playing a critical role. This book has been designed as a comprehensive reader for undergraduates and development practitioners, presenting the best of the now vast body of literature that has grown up alongside this acknowledgement. Five parts cover a review of the history of the theoretical debates, the status of women in the household and family, women in the global economy, the impacts of social changes on women's lives, and women organizing for change.

Contents

Women's Studies/Development
Hb 1 85649 141 2
Pb 1 85649 142 0
416pp Bibliography Index Royal

ECOFEMINISM AS POLITICS
Nature. Marx and the Postmodern
Ariel Salleh, Griffith University

This book explores the philosophical and political challenge of ecofeminism. It shows how the ecology movement has been held back by conceptual confusion over the implications of gender difference, while much that passes in the name of feminism is actually an obstacle to ecological change and global democracy. The author argues that ecofeminism reaches beyond contemporary social movements, being a political synthesis of four revolutions in one: ecology is feminism is socialism is post-colonial struggle.

Informed by a critical postmodern reading of the Marxist tradition, Salleh's ecofeminism integrates discourses on science, the body, culture, nature, political economy.

Contents

Women's Studies/Environment/Social Theory/Philosophy
Hb 1 85649 399 7
Pb 1 85649 400 4
224pp Notes Index Metric demy

GENDER AND CATASTROPHE
Edited by Ronit Lentin, Trinity College Dublin

This book explores the gendered and gendering effects of violence against women in extreme situations such as major wars, genocides, famines, slavery, the Holocaust, mass rape, and ethnic cleansing. The female experience of methodical genocidal rape in the former Yugoslavia, women's coerced participation in the Rwandan massacre, the comfort women system during World War II, the gendering of genocidal strategies during the Holocaust, nuclear testing in the Pacific and the reproduction 'policy' in Tibet are all integrated into a wider framework – a framework which uncovers the true consequences of identifying women as simultaneously sexual objects, transmitters of culture and symbols of the nation.

Contents

Women's Studies/Disaster Studies/Human Rights/Holocaust Studies
Hb 1 85649 445 4
Pb 1 85649 446 2
256pp Index Metric demy

SUBVERSIVE WOMEN
Women's Movements in Africa, Asia, Latin America and the Caribbean
Edited by Saskia Wieringa
Institute of Social Studies, The Hague

This important anthology of feminist writing brilliantly demonstrates the complexity and diversity of women's movements and organisations worldwide. The book opens with an analysis of women's history as subversion and the methodological aspects of feminist research projects. Individual contributors look at the experience of their own countries and explore 'feminism' as it is defined in the North and the South.

Contents
1. Women's history as subversion
2. Methods and power
3. The mainstream of the women's movement in Peru
4. Peru: Rebellion into action
5. The early women's movement in Trinidad and Tobago
6. Women and colonial policy in Jamaica
7. An experiment in popular theatre and women's history
8. Somalia: Poetry as a form of resistance
9. The state of the Women's Union 1971-1983 in Sudan
10. On the 'crisis' in the Sudanese women's movement
11. Masses of women - but where is the movement? (India)
12. Organising women tobacco workers in India
13. Matrilinearity and women's interests.

Women's Studies/Development Studies
Hb 1 85649 317 2
Pb 1 85649 318 0
288pp Index Bibliography Metric demy

EMPOWERMENT AND WOMEN'S HEALTH
Theory, Methods, and Practice
Jane Stein, University of North Carolina at Chapel Hill

What are the issues at stake in women's health and local political activism across the globe? In this major analysis of women's empowerment and its relationship to health, Jane Stein looks at the factors that determine success in the fight for better conditions, redistribution of power and control of resources. Linking the policies of international development with women's situations, the theories and research into women's health with the lives of individuals, this study offers a broad and cogent analysis of the web of factors that are relevant to health, and reveals connections, associations, and interactions that escape a more narrow attempt to isolate remediable causes.

'An incisive overview of relevant intellectual paradigms, perceptive assessments of theories about women's health, and a comprehensive blueprint for future programming, research and funding to improve women's health and well-being.'
– *Rebecca J Cook, Director of the International Human Rights Law Program, University of Toronto*

Contents

Women's Studies/Health/Development Studies
Hb 1 85649 463 2
Pb 1 85649 464 0
336pp Tables Index Metric demy

POWER, REPRODUCTION AND GENDER
The Intergenerational Transfer of Knowledge
Edited by Wendy Harcourt, Society for International Development

A major intervention into the study of gender, power and reproduction around
the world, this book explores issues of health, empowerment, sexuality and
reproductive rights - issues fundamental to the on-going international
development debate on population and gender.

Studying a wide variety of societies - all immersed in deep change due to the
impact of modernity on economic, political and social institutions - a
distinguished cast of contributors investigate knowledge transfer inter- and
intra-generationally in reproductive behaviour.

Contents
1. Power, reproduction and gender: an analytical contribution
2. Traditional knowledge, modern interventions and women's decision making
in rural Ghana
3. Competing ideologies: adolescence, knowledge and silences in Dar es
Salaam
4. Family structure and social change in a Punjab village
5. Female honor: reproductive rights for domestic workers in Rio de Janeiro,
Brazil
6. Globalization of the economy and changes in traditional.hierarchies for
migrant workers in Sri Lanka
7. Modernity and Motherhood in Switzerland
8. Feminist Research and Methodology: lessons to be drawn
9. Conclusions: responsibilities, possibilities and barriers

Women's Studies/Development Studies
Hb 1 85649 425 X
Pb 1 85649 426 8
240pp Tables Index Metric demy

THE WORLD OF WIDOWS
Margaret Owen, founder, Empowering Widows in Development

This book provides a global overview of the status of widows around the world. While much has been written about widows in the North, few attempts have been made to address the disadvantages of widows in the South. Neglected by social policy researchers, international human rights activists and the women's movement, the author shows why the status of the world's widows - legal, social, cultural, economic - is an urgent issue given the extent and severity of the discrimination against them.

Contents

Women's Studies
Hb 1 85649 419 5
Pb 1 85649 420 9
224pp Bibliography Index Metric demy

WAR IN THE BLOOD
AIDS and Culture in Southeast Asia
Chris Beyrer, John Hopkins University School of Hygiene and Public Health

From Thailand's open debate about and readiness to deal with its HIV problem to the relationship between the Burmese regime and the drug trade, this engaging and vivid book investigates the way that the HIV epidemic has taken its course in seven countries of Southeast Asia. The author shows how the cultural and political landscapes of these countries have affected the often devastating progress of the disease. The way that the epidemic has spread is seen as being vitally linked to the general condition of human rights in the societies, while being specifically mediated by sexual behaviour, drug use and the state of health care.

Both passionate and well-informed, this book is a labour of love that discusses the problems of the HIV epidemic while giving a personal, often intimate, and ultimately celebratory account of the author's own experience of Southeast Asia and asserting the real possiblity for affirmative action.

Contents

Cultural Studies/HIV and AIDS/Southeast Asia/Health
Hb 1 85649 531 0
Pb 1 85649 532 9
256pp Index Metric demy